Hugh McNeile Dyer

The West Coast of Africa

As Seen from the Deck of a Man-of-War

Hugh McNeile Dyer

The West Coast of Africa
As Seen from the Deck of a Man-of-War

ISBN/EAN: 9783743419032

Manufactured in Europe, USA, Canada, Australia, Japa

Cover: Foto ©Andreas Hilbeck / pixelio.de

Manufactured and distributed by brebook publishing software (www.brebook.com)

Hugh Mcneile Dyer

The West Coast of Africa

H.M.S. "Torch" manning and arming boats in the River Congo.

THE
WEST COAST OF AFRICA

AS SEEN FROM

THE DECK OF A MAN-OF-WAR.

BY THE LATE

COMMANDER HUGH McN. DYER, R.N.,

H.M.S. "TORCH."

J. GRIFFIN & CO.

(Publishers, by Appointment, to H.R.H. the Duke of Edinburgh,)

15, COCKSPUR STREET, | AND 2, THE HARD,
PALL MALL, LONDON. | PORTSEA, PORTSMOUTH.

1876.

PRINTED AT THE OFFICE OF THE PUBLISHERS

INTRODUCTION.

SOME apology may perhaps be needed for the publica-
tion of this little volume, at a time when other interests
have somewhat withdrawn public attention from the
affairs of the Gold Coast; but the vast, and almost unknown African continent, must no doubt always form
a subject of interest for those who believe that in the
development of its resources a wide field remains yet
to be opened up. To them, these pages of a Sailor's
Journal may perchance record some interesting facts,
before unknown. It was not, however, as a field of
Scientific research that the West Coast of Africa had
a special interest for Captain Dyer. For on that coast,
in the year 1851, he lost an elder brother—a Sub-
Lieutenant (then called, a "Mate"), of H.M.S. *Niger*,
under the command of Captain (now Rear-Admiral) Sir
Leopold Heath. Captain Dyer's brother was killed
whilst gallantly leading his boat's crew in an attack
on Lagos. The two brothers were in the same ship,
and on the death of the elder, the Admiralty promoted
Hugh Dyer on account of his brother's service.

In revisiting that region Captain Dyer felt that any
account of it which he could give to his friends at home
would have peculiar interest also for them.

Hence it was that on his return to England, on his
retirement from the Navy, he employed some of his

spare time, and gave occupation to his active mind, in preparing these pages. He did not, however, like to undertake the risk of publishing, and his sudden and early death soon after removed him from us.

His work is, therefore, now put forth in this form as a memorial of him, and it is commended to those who knew Hugh Dyer as a friend, a genial companion, and an officer, believing that all such will esteem it, not so much on account of any particularly striking information which it may contain, as that possibly in his Journal they may find something which will bring to their remembrance the warm heart and bright and kindly face which will never greet them again.

The Journal ends with the arrival of the *Torch* at Gibraltar, but Captain Dyer's subsequent deeds, after joining the Flag of Admiral Sir Hastings Yelverton, are not unknown to fame. These, however, he has modestly left unrecorded, but they may be here alluded to, as displaying in a marked manner his characteristic qualities. For without doubt his imperturbable coolness under exciting circumstances, and his happy combination of good nature and pluck, of readiness to fight, if fighting were necessary, or to fraternize if the same object could be peacefully gained, helped in no slight degree to secure that best of all results—a complete but bloodless victory." (See *Times* of 14th October, 1873).

The doings of "the plucky little *Torch* whose modest motto 'I show the way' was well earned at

Carthagena, were described at some length by the Special Correspondent of the *Times*, according to whom Captain Dyer, with a face full of good humour, frankness, and pluck, the beau ideal of an English Sailor's face, was smiling at the scowling crowd much as if he thought they were treating him to an 'ovation' which he did not quite understand, but still felt bound gratefully to acknowledge. The Spaniards clearly did not know what to make of him and slowly and sulkily gave way." (See *Times* of 19th August, 1873.)

Soon after these events, the retirement scheme of that year was brought out, and the advantages offered in it, induced Captain Dyer to accept them. Thus ended his career in the profession to which he was most warmly devoted, and (to quote once more from the *Times'* Correspondent, when alluding to the circumstance,) "the English Service lost an officer of a kind that no service can afford to lose."

He is now, alas, lost; not only to the Service, but to his friends also, and he will long be regretted by all who "knew him as a sincere friend, a pleasant companion and a first rate officer."

CONTENTS.

CHAPTER VI.

CHAPTER VII.

CHAPTER VIII.

CHAPTER IX.

The West Coast of Africa:

As seen from the Deck of a Man-of-War.

CHAPTER I.

N the 25th of September, 1871, I left Southampton in the Cape Mail Steamer *Cambrian*, to take command of H.M.S. *Torch* on the West African Station. Our voyage was one of incident and interest, and far from being altogether unpleasant, although few longer ones are on record. Mr. Boyle, in his book *"To the Cape for Diamonds,"* has given an account of it, which I will not repeat here; sufficient to say that we did, eventually, on the 8th November, of the same year, reach Table Bay! The *Cambrian* was a sister ship to Her Majesty's newly acquired ship *Dromedary, neé Briton,* and of about

B

equal speed. Proceeding at once to the naval head-
quarters at Simons' town, I found that the *Torch* had
been ordered to St. Helena by the 1st of December,
and I received orders to return there to meet her.

The old *Cambrian* was again my carrier, but as she
had a fair wind this time we made a quick passage of
three days, and I was only too glad to travel with my
old friends, Captain Diver and his officers.

On arrival at St. Helena, to our dismay we found
that we had to perform a four days quarantine, the
Cape being suspected of measles, by the island authorities. Local history stated that measles had on one or
two occasions played great havoc among the coloured
population, and was consequently greatly dreaded.
We passengers from the Cape had not heard of its
prevalence there. However, there was no getting over
the difficulty. I had one fellow sufferer, the Rev. J. J.
Beck, of D'Urban, Capetown. He and I fought and
begged for freedom without avail : for within an hour of
the *Cambrian's* departure we were landed bag and
baggage, on the rocks below Banks fort, three miles
east of Jamestown, with a key, which we were told
would open a door somewhere thereabout, within which
He should find shelter. Captain Diver in the most
thoughtful manner, had provided against our immediate
starvation by adding a well-filled basket to our luggage,
and he tried to raise our spirits with a hearty cheer
from his ship, by passengers and crew, as they passed

us. But our position was not a pleasant one. Our luggage was heavy, Mr. Beck was heavy too, and on the slippery rocks it was rather dangerous for him to move. I could not lift our boxes by myself, and the tide was flowing. I secured the light packages, and leaving Mr. Beck to watch the heavy ones, and amuse himself by shaking his stick at Jamestown and tell his grievances to the fast flowing waves, I scrambled up the rocks to look for assistance. Fortunately, I found some coloured men collecting guano, and pressed one of them into my service, by shaking hands with him, and informing him he was in quarantine for touching me, and he must come along. With his aid I secured the luggage, and Mr. Beck. We had a steep climb of about 300 feet, to some long disused military quarters. The key would not open any door we could find. A little pressure of our backs did. We found a couple of little barrack rooms in not bad repair and an iron bedstead in each. Our factotum brought our luggage up, and shortly afterwards appeared some furniture and more provisions from the Naval Agent at Jamestown, and a kind note from Mr. Moss offering services. Glad to find ourselves not altogether forgotten, and likewise made happy in finding our man of all work a fair cook, we gave ourselves fairly up to the situation and tried to make the best of it. Mr. Beck had come to see his son, who was on his way to England from Java, and had been landed on the island in what was supposed to

be a dying state, but happily our news was that he was
much better; although this was a great relief to Mr.
Beck's mind, yet he could not restrain from writing a
stream of expostulatory letters to the Governor and
other authorities, on the hardness of his case and
ridiculousness of their conduct. The letters evoked a
polite reply or two, but not one minute of our imprisonment was remitted. And such a prison to! On
the side of a cliff composed of cinders or volcanic
rubbish, without a vestige of herbage to relieve the
eye,—the sea below, and the sky above. No means of
taking exercise, and no escaping from the voracity of
the fleas indoors! I wonder what these lively animals
fed on before our arrival?

The *Torch* arrived the day before I was liberated;
as soon as that took place I went on board and relieved
Acting Commander Evans from his command. She is
one of the prettiest little ships in the Service but very
small — 428 tons. Her armament consists of four
20-pounder Armstrong breech-loaders, and one 64-
pounder muzzle-loader, with a complement of 67
officers and men and 12 Kroomen.

The mail from England arrived next day, and
brought Admiralty orders for the ship to go to the
Cape, so we had not much time to enjoy the hospitality
of St. Helena, but we soon learnt that it contained a
very pleasant society. A refreshing ride on the breezy
upland, among the English looking lanes with ripe

blackberries in the hedges, and roses blooming in the
gardens, enabled me to shake off the remembrance of
Banks', and I met Mr. Beck about to return to the
Cape in the mail steamer, in ecstasies of delight with
the courtesy and kindness he had received from the
Governor, the Colonial Surgeon, and everyone else in
the island, and not a word did he mention of quarantine or fleabites !

It is a wearisome passage to the Cape from St.
Helena, under sail, as foul winds prevail nearly all the
way. We were obliged to use as little steam as
possible, and did not arrive off the Cape before the
27th, having left St. Helena on the 5th December.
Just as we reached the " Bellows" rock off the Cape
point, round which we had to proceed to Simons' Bay,
a heavy gale came on, and with less than a mile to go
we had to bear up and run for shelter to Table Bay.
On the 29th we started again, and again a south-easter
prevented our rounding the Bellows, and we did not
reach Simons' Bay until the evening of the 31st.
During the two days we were struggling against a
heavy gale of wind and very high seas, and it seemed
as if we were doomed to play the " Flying Dutchman"
off the ever-blowing " Bellows."

The south-easters are the great drawback to Simons'
Town, for when they blow they render out-door
exercise next to impossible, as they carry not only
dust but sharp stones on their wings. I am sorry to

say they were very prevalent during our stay, which lasted until the 23rd February. This is a long and rare rest for a West Coast Cruizer, only to be accounted for by an exceptional circumstance. An important Court Martial had to be held on a late officer of the ship, and the Admiral commanding the Flying Squadron was ordered to sit as President. Admiral Seymour did not arrive until the 14th February.

Although the Cape and West Coast form one station, only the two Senior Officers' ships have much chance of seeing the Cape part of it. The coast squadron is so reduced that any other ship can rarely be spared.

We thoroughly appreciated our Cape visit, although the weather was not on its best behaviour, and the brown and yellow cheeks of the men who had been on the coast for the previous year became fresh and clear again.

Who has not heard of the charms of the Cape? Its society, its climate, its scenery, all delightful; but as they have been frequently described I cannot linger over them. We left Simons' Bay with many regrets and the most pleasing remembrance of our visit.

Our destination was the Congo. There we were to meet the Commodore. After passing Table Bay we caught another south-easter—this time a fair wind— which carried us our first thousand miles in four days; then the wind gradually died away, the water became smooth, and the weather warm but pleasant, and on the 8th March we anchored in the Congo. We had not sighted land during the passage although we were seldom more than 100 miles from it. We fell in with an American whaler off Great Fish Bay, eight months out and nearly full,—she was going across to Tristan d'Acunha to complete. We gave her a large bag of old newspapers, for which the mate who boarded us was very thankful.

The Congo is a grand river, without a bar or any obstruction to its entrance. It is in many places above Sharks Point more than 100 fathoms deep, and is navigable for vessels drawing 12 feet of water for 120 miles. Between Sharks Point on the south side and Banana on the north it is 7 miles wide, and it seldom narrows to less than a mile until far above M'Boma, which is 70 miles from Banana. The scenery on approaching the river from seaward is very pretty. Moderately high, green after the rains with the coarse grass it is clothed with, with groups of trees interspersed over it, the country has the appearance of English park land. Until the actual entrance of the river is reached, cliffs of a deep red colour form a margin to the green upland. Then come the mangrove and the swampy banks whereon it luxuriates.

The river enters the sea with great velocity, and its current is felt for more than 100 miles from the shore. The tide is seldom able to check it much, and sailing vessels have always had great difficulty in ascending it. Its waters are of a deep brown, and the curious spectacle of islands floating on its surface I have never seen elsewhere. These islands are of a considerable size, and have tall grass and sometimes shrubs growing on them. They have been met 300 miles at sea, still green. One that fell across our bows, when at anchor off Banana, was 10 feet deep and at least 150 feet long. They are formed by the strong current, during the heavy rains, tearing away the banks. We were now (March) in the middle of the rainy season, but although the rain fell heavily it seldom lasted long at a time.

We anchored at first off Banana, where most of the European factories are situated. Coal is generally to be obtained there, but the stock was out, so as Banana is unhealthy we moved over to Sharks Point, and anchored in very good shelter within 300 yards of it. Sharks Point is a low marshy peninsula, with a margin of sand towards the sea and river. A small clearance has been made among the mangrove trees, which come pretty close down, where a few native huts of cane are constructed, in which dwell some natives, who live by fishing and trading with ships that may anchor off the Point. Even during the slaving days our officers could land here, and the natives would furnish them with stock, and pretend to give them information of slaving operations in the river. They were soon on board of us with stock to sell and offers to do washing.

Each man wore some article of naval uniform, and was learned in at least a few words of African-English. Some of the certificates produced were remarkable, such as, "I certify John Thomas to be the greatest rogue on Sharks Point, but he is the best washerman. Don't pay him more than half-a-crown a dozen, and don't let him enter your cabin."

They generally find out if a certificate is altogether bad, and take care not to show it, but being thought a rogue is not with them such a bad character. John Thomas had served in a man-of-war, where he had eaten of the fruit of the tree of knowledge of good and evil, and with his native cleverness, made his own use of the power thus gained. The natives had all English names, and could tell stories about every ship that had visited Sharks point, and knew most of the officers that had ever been on the coast. They brought parrots and live stock to sell, and although purchases were nominally made in money, they were usually paid for in kind: old clothes, soap for the washerman, biscuit, &c., being in the greatest demand.

King Peter claimed the sovereignty of this dominion, as a vassal of King Antonio, whom he described to me as a magnificent prince of great power, but of whom more hereafter. He paid me an official visit, attended by a staff of two attendants, one bearing a large key to which was attached a piece of wood marked "Burial ground." He informed me that he kept the place clean where Englishmen were buried, and every Captain gave him a "Dash," that is a present. I declined giving the Dash until I had seen the ground. He begged hard for a salute, and I gave him, to his delight, one gun.

On visiting the shore I found the sand loose and tiresome to walk on, the paths through the grass wet and boggy. The little graveyard was under a large umbrella tree close to the landing, fenced round with the split stems of the palm leaf, and the graves kept tolerably clean. It was nearly full. Some of the head-boards were falling to decay, but many had been freshly renewed by ships which had lately been here. King Peter got his " Dash" with a warning not to fail in his agreement.

We lay here for nearly a fortnight, and the Commodore not arriving in that time we then proceeded to Kabenda, a port on the coast 30 miles north of the river and a healthier place to lay at. Here we found supplies plentiful, and the paths, which serve the purposes of roads everywhere in Africa, hard and wide, so that there were many pleasant walks to be taken. The sportsmen also found a little shooting at guinea fowl and franklin, although from the length of the grass they were difficult to get at : the best chance was at break of day among the cleared garden patches or fields of pea-nuts. Small bush deer abound, and the natives sometimes get them and sell the venison, which

is very good. The bright colour of the small birds was
very striking: scarlet and black, orange and black,
white and black, and pale blue prevailing. I heard a
few songsters among them.

There is a capital market held every morning under
a large tree close to an English factory. Barter appeared the only mode of exchange practised by the
natives. They seldom like to take money. Empty
bottles and soup tins will purchase fish, fruit or vegetables. A bottle would pay for 12 to 20 oranges. At
this time fruit was scarce. Fish in many varieties
could always be obtained. Among other kinds were
prawns and whitebait, or the fry of some fish, which
tasted quite as well.

Meat, such as beef and mutton, was scarce, but
could be obtained by giving a little notice; goats and
poultry were always obtainable, and the muscovy ducks
were especially good and cheap.

One of the most remarkable men in Kabenda is
" Capita," a native and relative of the King Chico
Franco. He has for many years acted as local agent
for the African Company of Merchants, whose head
quarters are at Banana, and I was told by Mr. Capper,
had always been found trustworthy, intelligent, and
painstaking. He cannot read or write, so he had
a Sierra Leone clerk to keep his accounts, but he
had been in England, and spoke English fairly.

He was not deeply impressed with the blessings of

civilization which he observed in our land, and told a
pitiable story of his sufferings in Liverpool, where he
had fallen among thieves, been robbed, ill treated, and
laughed at, and gave it as his opinion " England good
for white man, Kabenda good for black man ; you likee
England, you go ; I likee Kabenda, I stay." Capita had
always a good humoured smile about him, and was ever
ready to be of use to us, or to give information. He
was very rich, had many wives, and two or three
country houses, within a mile of Kabenda, built of
wood in more than usual native style. He wisely ad-
hered to the native dress, but it was always of good
material ; and native dresses, although they only consist
of a shirt and loin cloth, are often very expensive. He
wore a valuable ring on his finger, and would do his
sporting (stalking sparrows !) with a double barrelled
breech-loader of the latest fashion.

The Kabenda men are all a superior race for the
coast. They are expert sailors, and navigate the coast-
ing craft employed in collecting produce between St.
Paul's de Loando and the Gaboon. Many of them are
fair carpenters, coopers, blacksmiths, and tailors ; and
their towns and villages are the neatest and cleanest
to be seen anywhere. The houses are built of cane,
and thatched with palm leaves ; the space around each
is kept cleanly swept, and the gardens are regularly
laid out and well cultivated. Little ornamental plots
are even sometimes attempted, containing shrubs and

flowers. The women, as is the custom throughout
Africa do all this work, no freeman ever tilling the
ground, but the men build the houses, work at trades,
and as labourers at factories, and are seldom idle except
they have made sufficient money, when they will lay
basking in the sun, smoking a pipe made from a
calabash, and drinking rum like a "fine young nigger
gentleman, one of the modern day!"

The crops cultivated are pea-nut, cassada, Indian
corn, and harricot beans. The pea-nuts are grown for
exportation, the remainder for home consumption. The
export trade is in palm oil and pea-nuts; it is considerable and increasing.

Minerals are brought to market in small quantities,
but the chiefs have a prejudice against selling them,
they fear the greedy white man might take their
country from them if they knew how full of wealth it
is! Cotton has been grown, and was of good staple,
but the expense of production was too great. I don't
see why that should be, but these matters are not
easily understood. The country abounds in useful hard
woods, red and white. Orange, lime, mango, and guava
trees bear well, and the palm, of many varieties,
flourishes.

It is a pretty sight to see the fishing canoes go to
sea with the land breeze every morning. They are
small "dug outs," seldom with more than one man in
each, who propels his ship with a single paddle, with

which he also steers when he puts up a light spritsail of native cloth, made from palm fibre. As the canoes get out to sea they are so low as to be lost sight of, and the men seem to be standing on the water. They return with the sea breeze which usually sets in about noon and lasts until sunset. This breeze is very refreshing, and seldom strong enough to be disagreeable.

The maximum height of the Thermometer during March and April at Kabenda and the Congo was 89° under the awnings on board, and the minimum was 73°. Heavy rain fell on seven days during our stay.

On the 5th of April we returned again to the Congo to meet the mail steamer. Whilst at anchor off Banana, I received a complaint from Mr. Capper, Agent for the Company of African Merchants, that a boat of his, manned by Kabenda men and bound up the Congo, had been boarded by pirates, robbed, some of the crew murdered, and others carried away into captivity. Having examined the survivors of the crew on oath— the native oath was taken after kissing the ground— we proceeded up the river in hope of surprising the pirates and obtaining hostages for the return of the prisoners. Having started at night, we arrived at the place, pointed out by the Kabenda men, at dawn ; and Lieutenant Jeffreys, with the armed boats of the ship, and accompanied by white interpreters and Kabenda men, started with orders to obtain redress for the outrage, or punish the tribe. The ship remained in the river opposite Sherwood Creek, up which the boats ascended. They had much further to go than was anticipated before they reached a village. They landed unexpectedly, and at first the natives seemed inclined to palaver. They were only gaining time for their women to escape to the bush with their household gods, and as soon as they calculated that was done, they themselves stampeded. Lieutenant Jeffreys tripped a chief up with his foot and held him as prisoner, but he forbade firing on the runaways, until he found his attempt at peaceful negociation entirely unavailing. This he shortly did, his hostage—the captive chief—making a sudden start between the legs of the too confident sentry and reaching his brethren in the bush in safety. Then, the sun getting high, and armed natives appearing in gathering force, other measures became necessary. Three villages were burned, the crops destroyed, a dozen canoes broken, and the expedition returned to the ship without a casualty. Quinine was served out, a good fresh meat dinner and a pint of beer each given to the men, and after a few hours rest they were as fresh as ever. I believe strict attention to diet and clothing is the great secret whereby men are kept in health on the coast.

It is of course necessary to punish pirates, but I cannot say the mode we are obliged to take is satisfactory to me. Burning a native town is not to be compared to the burning a town in our country, the houses can be built up again in a few days, but still it is a severe measure; and as I gained experience on the coast I thought I saw the way to inaugurate a new system, more consonant with our British principles and Christian name. We want a consul on this part of the coast, as we have in the Bights of Benin and Biafra, who not being a trader would be free from trade jealousies, and able to enter into relations with the more powerful of the river chiefs, who alone can stop piracy and other interferences with trade. It has been done elsewhere and can be done here. Unfortunately the Congo trade is chiefly in the hands of the Dutch, French, and Portuguese. An English consul would be looked upon with jealousy by them, but along the extent of coast from Ambriz to the Bights, English traders largely preponderate, and their trade is daily becoming more extensive and important.

On the 10th of April we returned to Kabenda, and on the 14th the *Rattlesnake* arrived, and we received orders to go to Cape Coast Castle, calling at Corsico Bay and Fernando Po, and we sailed the next day. We kept close along shore, making slow progress under sail with light winds. The country was green and pretty all along, sometimes the hills in the interior rose to the dignity of mountains, until we approached Cape Lopez, when we came to the mangroves, and low-lying land again—near here the Nazereth, Camma, and other rivers, said by some to be connected with the

Gaboon, debouch into the sea. North of the Gaboon the mountains appear again, and Corisco Bay is as lovely a spot as eye can rest upon. It is of considerable extent, perhaps 20 miles from north to south, and 15 miles deep from west to east. It is studded with islands, Corisco Island and numerous reefs off it sheltering the bay from seaward. Two large rivers, the Muni on the east, and the Moondah on the south side, enter it. The Elobey Islands are chosen as the trading station, and there is an American Missionary Station on Corisco Island.

The Bay is situated in 1° North Latitude, the climate is pleasant, but they have rather more than the coast average of rain, and at this season are occasionally visited by a sharp tornado.

The object of our visit was to enquire into circumstances connected with the loss of the Mail Steamer *Macgregor Laird*. She still remained on the rock on which she struck, about a mile from the North entrance to the bay, near Cape St. John. The natives have a somewhat Cornish idea of wrecks, and consider them "godsends" for their especial benefit. The cargo of the steamer just suited them. She was on her outward voyage, and full of the usual trade goods. Such good luck had never happened before and was never likely to happen again. The Captain and crew were glad to escape with their lives to Elobey, the former having previously sold ship and cargo to a speculative trader for £500.

C

This gentleman thought he had great interest with the natives, and telling them he would give them all that was in the forehold, he sat on the main hatch, and said what was beneath that, he should keep for himself. The natives agreed to this arrangement until the forehold was emptied, when they requested the patient speculator to move, and emptied the mainhold too. However, I expect he covered his first outlay by the ship's furniture he recovered after the natives had finished.

But retribution followed. The Spanish Government claim Corisco Bay as a dependency of Fernando Po. On the Governor hearing of the wreck he sent a gunboat, and one of our vessels, the *Bittern*, also appeared with the British Consul on board. The chiefs were summoned to restore the goods, and this not being complied with, every town and village in the vicinity was burnt, and the Corisco Islands condemned to pay a fine of 1,000 dollars. The amusing part of this business was that the fine was paid in goods stolen from the *Macgregor Laird!*

Previous to this occurrence the Spaniards had not kept any officials in Corisco Bay, but now a boat was left at Elobey with four or five sailors, who were armed with percussion muskets, for which caps could not be obtained.

We anchored near the Elobey Islands; the factories are on the smaller one, and no natives are allowed to live on the island, but they come there daily to trade. There are also some trade hulks at the entrance of the river Muni in a well sheltered and convenient position.

My enquiry was relative to an attack upon the crew of the *Macgregor Laird*, after they had landed from the wreck; also into an outrage committed upon Dr. Walker, an agent for the company of African merchants, some months before.

The first case was a simple one. One of the ship's Kroomen had a dispute with a native woman. A small beginning had a serious ending, and the natives taking the woman's part, took up their guns against the Kroomen, who joined their comrade; firing commenced, and the shot struck some of the white men of the crew accidentally; the Krooman who commenced the quarrel was most to blame.

Relative to Mr. Walker's complaint some curious matter cropped up. It seems the crew of a Spanish gunboat landed under arms, to protect the Judge who was going to enquire into his complaint against a Chief. The natives got frightened, and thought they were going to be attacked, ran to the bush for their guns, which frightened the Spaniards; they bolted for their boats at once, and made off to their ship, the Captain sending Mr. Walker a message through a pilot, that if he wished, he would bombard the island, but he could not risk his men's lives on shore again! Mr. Walker politely declined the offer, as he and his fellow-

C 2

countrymen would be the only sufferers by such a proceeding. The natives then tried to burn Mr. Walker's house which with great difficulty he prevented. In escaping from the island at night he was nearly killed, and his cooper, who accompanied him, was mortally wounded. Mr. Walker had offended the natives in some matter of trade, and the attack upon him appeared to be a *personal* matter, and not against Europeans generally. One of the men who had attacked him, was a prisoner at Fernando Po for the offence, but the Spaniards had very little power to maintain order at this place, and had much better not attempt to do so. The trade is in dye woods and India rubber. A few sundries occasionally are offered, and there is every prospect of a large trade here when the Muni is opened up, and the interior reached by our merchants. All the coast tribes are brokers to the trade, they do not produce much themselves, but buy from those that do so, and pay in the goods they get from European merchants on credit. Of course these people object to our dealing directly with the tribes in the interior, for then their occupation will be gone, and from this cause come many little wars, and many of those difficulties which our guns are requested to settle.

I was told a circumstance here that rather surprised me. In the defence of his house, Mr. Walker wounded a chief. The tribe claimed blood money from all the

H.M.S. "Torch" in a Tornado.

white traders on the island, as Mr. Walker had escaped ; and it was paid. The fine amounted to some pound or two a-piece. It seems you may do almost anything to a native but draw his blood—chain him up, flog him, abuse him if he offends as much as you like, but don't make his nose bleed !

The canoes in this bay are the neatest made of any I have seen, and they go along at a great pace, they are often extremely small, just sufficiently buoyant to float a man.

On our way to Fernando Po we encountered a very severe tornado. It gave the usual warning of its approach, and all sail was furled ere it struck us. First there were the heavy clouds to leeward, and lightning. Then the deep black arch, under which appeared a line of white foam a few minutes before it reached us, then the hissing noise as it came close, the shock and reel of the ship as it struck, and the crackling thunder, vivid lightning and deluge of rain, gradually growing less, until, in half-an-hour we were in fine weather again, and the air all the cooler for the squall.

The scenery is lovely about Fernando Po. The island is only 20 miles distant from the main land, its highest point is 10,000 feet above the sea, and it is clad in magnificent trees nearly to the summit. Opposite, on the mainland, are the Cameroon mountains 14,000 feet high, the range extending far into the interior.

The only town on Fernando Po is on the north side of the island. The Governor-General and his staff reside there. His Excellency is commander of the small vessel of war stationed here, and nearly all the officers of the island also belong to this ship. The town consists of about 50 houses, most of them built of wood and many in a dilapidated condition. It has seen better days. The island is capable of producing almost anything, but actually produces very little. Some very good cocoa is grown by a Spanish gentleman, but only on a limited scale, as an experiment.

The natives are a very low type of humanity, the lowest I have ever seen. They are dreadfully dirty. They are not allowed to enter the town without some kind of clothing, which sometimes consists of a small apron, or even a pat of cow dung tied to their waists by a bit of string. They are useless as labourers, and Kroomen have to be imported for this purpose.

It is possible to get a good long walk on a hard wide path, under the shade of the trees, which often rise to a great height and spread their branches over head in the kindest possible manner, but this can only be done in the morning and evening, the mid-day heat being intense. It is advisable for any person with a ship to go to, to sleep on board; those who live on shore are very subject to fever, and although coast fever is not usually of a character fatal to life, it is always trying to the temper and wearing to the constitution. Where-

ever I paid a visit on the Coast, I always found the conversation in a very short time turn upon fever, and it
was looked upon by many as a necessary evil which
must come sooner or later. Some speak of it as our
mothers do of the measles, and other ailments children
are supposed to be the better for having early in life; if,
they say, you get fever, after escaping from it for a year
or two after coming to the country, so much the worse
for you.

One thing I am sure of, people who are always
dosing themselves are the less able to bear the attack
when it comes on. About quinine as a preventive, I
am not sure. Our men used to take small doses, two
grains morning and evening when in the rivers, and we
had very little fever among them, and never lost a man;
but it certainly affects the head, and is apt to induce
deafness. A gentleman at Fernando Po told me he
never took quinine, except when he felt fever coming
on, when he took 20 grains, and was all right next day.

After coaling, we sailed on the 30th April for Cape
Coast, touching at Jellah Coffee for supplies. We had
light winds, with occasional tornadoes and showers of
heavy rain on the passage; the water was smooth and
there was not much current. From Cape Palmas to
Fernando Po, the Guinea current runs almost constantly
to the east in a line with the coast, and between
Palmas and Cape St. Paul attains at times great
velocity. The wind at the same time being south-

westerly, it is very difficult for a ship under sail to get
to the westward if she stays in shore; but a little
further off is another current, the Equatorial, which
runs counter to the Guinea current, only not with equal
force. During this passage we found both wind and
current out of their normal condition, and we reached
Jellah Coffee in eight days under sail. We arrived at
a fortunate moment. The homeward mail steamer was
expected, and a dozen large canoes full of stock were in
the roads waiting for her. They came on board of us
as soon as we anchored, and marketing on a lively scale
was soon going on in our gangways and forecastle.
Permission having been given, there was a great rush
to be first on board, and all were anxious to bring as
much as possible with them. A dozen ducks tied by
the legs in a bundle, balanced a dozen fowls, carried
over the shoulder ; a pig under the left arm, a
basket of pea nuts or chillies in the mouth, and the
right arm and feet alone free to scramble on board with.
There was great excitement and jabbering when a pig
and duck escaped into the sea and swam in different
directions,—the owner sprang after them, but had no little
trouble in catching them, especially piggy. Turkeys
weighing six pounds to nine pounds, cost four shillings
each. Chickens small, four shillings a dozen. Ducks ten
shillings a dozen. Pine apples three-pence each. Yams,
onions, chillies, cocoa nuts and pea-nuts cheap and
plentiful, the little onions—shallots, being very good.

Mr. August, an educated native, is a contractor to supply the navy with fresh beef, which he does at the rate of £2 5s. per bullock. The animals are small, averaging about one hundred pounds of beef, but the meat is good. Sheep and goats are to be had, but the former are comparatively dearer than bullocks. King Tay, an old friend of the English, is the chief over these people, and he has become rich from this provision trade. Jellah Coffee is close to the old English fort of Quittah, at present abandoned, although within the Gold Coast protectorate. It is situated on a low strip of sand, on which grow a few bushes, between the sea and a large lagoon in connection with the river Volta, and the numerous lakes which stretch along the coast to the westward towards Whydah; so that its water communication, with the more inland country is very great, and being a known market for all kinds of fresh stock, it finds its way there. The landing is not good, and I did not attempt it. There is nothing to be seen to invite one to risk a wetting, except a comfortable looking German factory built close to our ruined fort at Quittah.

CHAPTER II.

We anchored off Cape Coast Castle at daylight on the 10th April. The roadstead is quite open to the prevailing wind, and a swell is always rolling in from seaward, rendering landing difficult and dangerous, except in boats specially adapted for the purpose. As the current runs along the shore, vessels lay with their broadsides to the swell, and roll heavily and uncomfortably. More crockery was broken on board the *Torch*, whilst at anchor off the Gold Coast, than during all the rest of the time I was in her.

From the sea, Cape Coast Castle is quite an imposing looking place, with its large fort, public buildings, and comfortable looking private residences perched on the high ground. The surrounding country was green and well wooded, and of an undulating character. Elmina was clearly in sight to the west some eight miles distant.

The surf boats used for landing passengers or cargo, are large and wide, shaped like a life boat with both ends alike, and rising higher at the bow and stern than in the middle. They are rowed by from ten to sixteen natives with short paddles. The paddlers sit on the gunwhale of the boat, and when they like, make her go along very fast with the short and quick digs they make at the water. The steersman uses an oar, and stands up in the stern to give directions. He makes use of violent language to the crew when he wants to get in advance of an approaching breaker; and these men are as a rule very clever in handling their boats.

The men don't appear able to pull without singing, and with passengers they take care to improve the occasion, and give the burden of their song a practical application, thus :—

> " Mama come again, come again, come again,
> Captain, good man, dash we dollar ;
> 'Spose he dash we, we no wet him.
> Mama come again, come again, come again.
> Captain, rich man ; nigger, poor man.
> Four five shillings dash poor black man.
> Hib, hib, hurrah ! God blessee you."

and so on all the way to shore, striking the gunwhale occasionally with their paddles to mark the time. " Dash" in African parlance means a present, the equivalent of backsheesh. On approaching the shore the men paddle easily until the steersman sees a good opportunity for a comparative smooth, when he gives the order to give way, and the men with a low sup- pressed " hi," " hi," " hi," dig away as hard as they can with their paddles until the boat touches the shore, when every man jumps overboard, and before the next wave can reach her have carried her as far as they are.

able up the beach; passengers are carried out, cargo
removed, and the boat rolled over and over to a place
of safety beyond the reach of the surf.

In embarking the contrary operation takes place.
The boat is turned over and over on its broadside until
it reaches the margin of the water, then it is loaded
with cargo, its bow pointed seaward, and passengers
carried into their places. Each man then sees his
paddle in its place and stands outside the boat opposite
it, waiting orders. The Padron, or coxswain, watches
the rollers, which vary in height at intervals. The
boat is pushed as far into the water as can be done
without setting her afloat, until a favourable opportunity arrives, when with great clatter of tongues,
and all the bodily energy they can use, the boat is
pushed afloat, the men jump up and work away with a
"hi, hi, hi," until the outer breaker is passed, when
they take it easy again and strike up a song. It has a
very intimidating effect upon the uninitiated, to be in
one of these boats as she nears a breaker six or eight
feet high above the boat, and apparently coming right
into her. But the boats rise in a wonderful manner,
and a skilful Padron will generally avoid seas as high
as six feet, although I have seen the boats turn right
over on end. Of course this is very·dangerous, but
it is a·point of honour with the crews not to let a
white passenger drown if it is possible to save him,
and they are all expert swimmers.

Cape Coast stands on ground about 150 feet above the level of the sea, its streets are wide and well macadamized, the principal ones being lined on each side with trees: brick drains built at the side to carry off the water during the heavy rains. The houses occupied by Europeans and well-to-do natives, are large and airy, and adapted to the climate. They are built of clay, whitewashed, and shaded by balconies and green verandahs. Government House is commodious and comfortable, and during even the hottest part of the day it was not difficult to find a pleasantly cool corner within its hospitable walls.

Mr. Ussher, the Administrator, or Lieutenant-Governor, had been many years on the Gold Coast, and unfortunately at this time was not in good health, which was a great misfortune to him, as the transfer of the Western districts to us from the Dutch, had just taken place. However, Mr. Pope Hennessy, the Administrator-in-Chief was at Elmina. Mr. Ussher had formed a pretty garden in front of his house, full of bright flowers, and what was still more pleasing to the eye, a piece of emerald green lawn, where he had made a croquet ground. There were no white ladies at Cape Coast at this time, but tradition told of a small gathering of them at his Excellency's croquet parties. Mrs. Ussher had lived some time there. Of course the climate is trying to English ladies, but I cannot think it is nearly so much so as that of Bengal.

The cool refreshing sea breeze that sweeps through the Cape Coast verandahs every afternoon, has no equivalent on the Indian plains. Nothing is so much missed on the West African Station as ladies' society, and persons knowing the country can understand how much good a few cheerful energetic ladies would do among their countrymen at such places as Cape Coast. I met a few native ladies of colour, at a government house croquet party, of pleasant manner and conversation, but I believe there are but few of them. There is a great lack of any means of relieving the monotonous official or business life an European has to lead here, by out-door amusements. There is a little shooting, and now and then a cricketing eleven can be raised, to play a match with the officers of a man-of-war ; but horses do not thrive, it is even said they will not live, and the climate is against much walking exercise. A few vehicles are kept by members of the upper ten—not thousand, but individuals—in which they take an airing. These are drawn by natives, and it is very tame work,—nearly as much so as being wheeled about in a bath chair. There was only one road worthy of the name leading out of Cape Coast along which a walk could be taken, but several hard tracks or paths, and a road to Elmina was just being commenced at this time.

Cape Coast markets are not good, they are irregularly supplied, comparatively dear, and the poultry and meat is inferior. Our contractor for the supply of fresh beef procured his cattle from Sierra Leone; they were much finer beasts than those at Jellah Coffee, but the beef was not much better,—vegetables were very scarce. There was no reason for this, for the soil will produce abundance, and exceedingly good vegetables are grown in private gardens.

There are no shops, after the English sort, in the town; but several stores, where all articles in native demand can be obtained, and wines, tinned meats, and groceries.

A steamer from England arrives every week, thus a stock of supplies can easily be kept up.

The chief occupation of the people appeared to me to be net making and fishing. The nets used were cast nets, which are thrown very expertly among the shoals of herrings—or a fish very like a herring with more bones than usual—which frequent the coast. The boats used for fishing differ from the surf boats; they are narrow, with the fore end covered in, carry two or three men each, but are equally convenient to get through the surf as the large boats, except that you may be sure of a wetting if you take a passage in one. Fishing is carried on with hand lines and long lines also, and the boats go miles out to sea, fishing in fine weather. There is one day in the week, Tuesday I think it is, on which they will not fish for some religious reason.

There are a great many native people in Cape Coast who dress in European style, but by far the majority adhere to the old and more picturesque mode of loin-cloth—or at any rate that and a shirt. I have heard the terms "clouty man" and "trowser man" used to define members of different classes of society. The "clout" consists of a piece of coloured cotton cloth folded round the loins; the women let it hang below the knee, and often add a short chemise or another cloth round their shoulders, but West African natives are never seen after the age of childhood without some kind of clothing. Ladies may be surprised to hear that "chignons" and "paniers" were worn in this country before they were dreamt of at home. I never walked through the streets of Cape Coast, without seeing women seated in front of their doors doing up their hair in fantastic shapes, such as a balloon behind, or two high pads, or horn shaped erections; then for the "paniers," they were always hidden from sight by the covering cloth, but I have been confidentially informed they are made of basket work, and their supposed use, to carry the baby on; for infants are always carried by their mothers on the hip, Indian fashion, or behind; but the effect of this machine on the walk of these women is ludicrous. They are fond of ornaments and wear bracelets and bangles of silver, copper, iron, or beads, as they can afford them, and often have gold ornaments in their hair. Cape Coast jewellers are

very clever, some of them doing as good and well
finished work as the Maltese, and it is very much
cheaper. They have not many patterns, but they are increasing them, and they are very expert copyists, if not
inventors, so that they seldom see a new design without
improving their style of work. Very handsome neck-
laces and bracelets are made by setting the green
beetle in heavy gold filagarce work. These are not,
however, for native wear, but are made for Europeans
who order them. Native ornaments take a more solid
form, but show considerable artistic skill in design and
construction. The gold used is that found in the
country, with very small quantity of alloy, except it is
intended to deceive an innocent stranger, where more
alloy than gold may be found in the pretty looking
article. It is always well to consult an European resident before making purchases of jewellery.

Mr. Ussher had a very fine puff adder, eight feet in
length, in a cage in his verandah. It had been
captured in the neighbourhood, and the natives brought
all such prizes to the Governor knowing him to be a
collector. It was in perfect health and very lively, its
strike was so rapid that the eye could not catch it, and
was only recognised by the thump of the animal's head
against the wires of the cage. Snakes, I was told,
abounded in the bush, some of large size; the Governor
told me of a large black one he encountered on his
return from a walk, that had entwined its tail round a

D

tree standing in the middle of the road, a tolerably
wide one, and moved its head about as he tried to pass
on either side to prevent it, so that he had to go back
and get home another way. I have seen very large
"tom-toms," native drums, at least twelve inches in
diameter covered with snake skin, but much as I have
walked in African bush I never saw a live snake there.
There are some beautifully coloured lizards in the
country and certain species attain great size. The
chameleon is common. I was not troubled much with
mosquitoes and in no part of the coast have I found
these little torments so numerous or so venomous as
elsewhere—Calcutta or Bermuda for instance.

I tasted palm wine for the first time here. This
popular native beverage is obtained by making an incision in the palm tree close to the new wood, inserting
a short stick in the incision and hanging a calabash to
catch the juice as it flows. The operation is generally ·
performed in the evening and the calabash removed in
the morning, when the wine, drank fresh, is really
pleasant and refreshing, and quite wholesome. If
allowed to ferment, which it will do in a few hours, it
becomes intoxicating in its effects and very dangerous
to the health of Europeans ; but the natives like it
best thus, and drink large quantities of it. I believe
if rain falls while the juice is flowing it spoils the
wine. The taste is something like cocoa-nut milk, only
slightly acid.

On the 20th May we moved to Elmina, where his Excellency the Administrator-in-Chief and Mrs. Pope Hennessy were residing. The fort of St. George is a very substantial building standing upon several acres of ground. It is entered by a drawbridge over a deep ditch faced with strong masonry. Within, it contains large barracks, stores, official residences, workshops, and courtyards. On its walls are cannon of different calibre, but mostly of very antiquated pattern. Here Mr. Hennessy had taken up his quarters, not in the most elegantly furnished apartments I have seen, even on the coast, or surrounded by many luxuries or even comforts, but his own official residence is at Sierra Leone, and he had come to Elmina to work, and such matters did not appear to trouble him. But other things did. Elmina and the western district of the protectorate as far as Appolonia had been taken over from the Dutch in April. The government of Holland had sent a " Dash" to their late *employés* at Elmina on leaving. Some discontent had arisen with regard to the proceedings of Lieutenant Joorst, the Dutch officer charged with distributing the money, and a riot had occurred after Elmina came under our protection, in which Mr. Joorst had been murdered, and the murderers had not been found.

The Dutch Commodore was on shore when the murder took place, and had complained that our authorities had not done their duty, so our Governor had cause to be troubled, but he was determined to discover the murderers, and had told the King at palaver, that they must be handed over to justice.

There are—or were—two towns at Elmina: the King's town consisting entirely of native houses, built of clay, and thatched with palm leaves; they are very close together, and many of them of two stories. Divided from it by the river Beyrah, is the Garden town containing many respectable slated houses and a Wesleyan church. Its streets are not so wide or clean as Cape Coast, or its stores so good. Overlooking it is Fort St. Jago, bright with whitewash, and surrounded by green bushes and growing crops. The gardens and fields around Elmina appeared to be better cultivated than those at Cape Coast, but the effect of the late war between these rival towns, had been, I was told, to throw a large quantity of ground out of cultivation.

Sanitary measures were certainly worse attended to by the Dutch than by our officers. The smells even in the fashionable quarter of Elmina were fearful, and in no African town have my nose and eyes been so offended as on the beach or beneath the castle walls of this town. Refuse of every kind is emptied there and left for the tide to wash away, which it is not always as quick in doing as might be wished. Mangy looking dogs rove about the streets, and the place is as full of long legged black pigs as a West Cork town on a fair day. Woe to those who indulge in pork!

There are one or two houses, calling themselves
"Hotels" in the town, only it is well not to expect too
much, or anything quickly, at these establishments.
Mrs. Last, who kept the one I visited, was the widow
of an ex-Dutch governor, or rather of several ex-
Dutch governors, and had a son bearing a commission
in the Army of His Majesty the King of the Nether-
lands. A widow! I must explain. It has been a
recognised custom between the Dutch and the native
tribes whom they protected, that Europeans should
take to themselves a wife from the natives, the marriage
ceremony to be according to native customs, the wife
to have legal rights during the stay of the white man
in the country, and the children considered legitimate.
Mrs. Last's husbands had not all died, but had returned
to Holland! I never heard an expression against the
morality of this institution ; and of course it ought to
be viewed very much from a local point. Certainly
country wives did not look upon themselves as the
white men's mistresses.

Mrs. Last baked beautiful bread and made delicious
sponge cakes, with which, and bitter beer—at half-a-
dollar a bottle—she entertained us, but, for mutton
chops, or even bacon and eggs, I am afraid we might
have waited until, from free use of sponge cake, our
appetite had departed.

Although we had only possessed Elmina for one
month, there was not a child in the place who could

not say "Give me a penny." Poor Mrs. Last was
more troubled with having to change her European
language from Dutch to English, than any other matter
connected with the transfer, although naturally she was
ill satisfied with the departure of her Dutch friends, and
the little chance she had of ever reigning again in
Fort St. George; but even she had mastered our
language to a considerable extent so as to be able to
carry on her business. She had been entrusted with
the preparation of a banquet to be given by His
Excellency, Governor Hennessy, on the anniversary of
Her Majesty's birthday, and was in great delight at
this honour having been conferred upon her, and
promised to astonish us with some wonderful produc-
tions of her confectionary art.

The forts were garrisoned with Houssa troops, and
the streets patrolled by Fantee police. Both these
bodies have been heard of by the public, during the
present Ashantee war. The police are recruited in the
country, wear a blue uniform, and carry a truncheon in
the streets, but have rifles and bayonets ready in the
barracks. The Houssas are a Mahomedan tribe living
to the east, and inland, on the banks of the Niger.
They are slight, active, soldierly looking men, dressed
in dark blue blouse and short trowsers of dungaree
trimmed with red braid, and a little red cap worn in a
jaunty cavalry style on the side of their head: they did
not wear shoes or stockings. They used English

words of command at their drill, but understood very
little more of the language. The non-commissioned
officers looked very proud of their stripes. One evening we were very much amused at witnessing a dance
given by the Houssas, as an entertainment to a few co-
religionists, if not clansmen, who lived in the interior,
and had come in to pay our soldiers a visit. A ring
was formed in the open space opposite the gate of Fort
St. George, by hosts and guests, men and women, sitting
on the ground. The music consisted of two drums and
a cow's horn, playing no particular tune. First a man
got up, and swung his arms, body, and legs about—the
legs least of all; then a woman joined him, then more
men and women all acting independently, except that
they generally went round the ring in one direction.
The sergeant-major's wife appeared to be doing the
honours. She was a stout lady arrayed in a black
velvet cloth, and showed her attention to her lady
friends, by stepping into the ring, when she observed
them getting warm, and wiping them down with a
large bandana handkerchief! I never saw people so
thoroughly enjoying themselves. There appeared to be
many advantages in this native dance, over our English
ones. No one waited to be asked to dance by a
partner, or risk the disappointment of finding the lady
of his choice pre-engaged. Everyone got up, when so
disposed, performed what antics he or she liked, and
sat down when tired. There was no weariness, no

wall-flowers, no supper, no indigestion, no headaches
next morning, and I hardly think it possible there could
have been any future scandal consequent upon flirta-
tions.

I suppose the music given at this ball was considered
as that most likely to be appreciated by the Houssa's
guests, for later in the evening I heard the very nice
little drum and fife band of the corps, playing " Coming
thro' the rye," " Cheer boys cheer," and other airs, remarkably well.

Mr. Hennessy entertained us in the Castle, on the
Queen's birthday, at dinner. All the heads of depart-
ments were present, several coloured gentlemen among
them,—one of these was Mr. Maxwell the Colonial
Chaplain, and another the Assistant Colonial Engineer.
Mrs. Last did her duty womanfully, and several of her
dainty dishes were highly appreciated, although, as she
led us to expect, she excelled in confectionary. We
had of course the usual loyal toasts and consequent
speeches, in which the Governor told us that Admiral
de Ruyter's baton had always been kept in the Castle
of St. George since that old enemy of ours on the sea,
had died ; and that it had been handed to him by the
Dutch governor to signify the transfer of the fort, but
that with the concurrence of the home government he
proposed returning it to Holland.

Three natives had been handed over to the police by
the king as the perpetrators of Mr. Joorst's murder, and

were to be tried before our Judge, with a native jury, at Elmina.

In the evening we had a grand display of fireworks from the castle walls to amuse the natives. I rather think the rockets frightened them, and some of us feared for those thatched roofs, which have since shown how quickly they will burn, and how impossible it would have been to have arrested the progress of a fire on the south side of the Beyrah.

We took several long walks during our stay. Except a day or so after heavy rain the roads were hard and pleasant to walk on, and the scenery lovely. We never received anything but civility from the natives, although some of our officers went four or five miles into the interior in their rambles. The weather was not overpoweringly hot, the thermometor averaging about 85° in the shade in midday, and 75° at night. The cool sea breeze is felt as well here as at Cape Coast, and between 4 p.m. and 7 p.m., or early in the morning a walk was very enjoyable. We saw several herds of fat, well conditioned, little cattle, but were told their owners considered them " fetish," or holy, and would not kill them, except for a " consideration." Goats, poultry, and eggs, bread, milk and fresh fish, in several varieties—even soles, were the provisions ordinarily obtainable in the market, with vegetables and fruit.

Hucksters sat at stalls under the shade of the trees

in the streets, selling cassada, kanky, snails, gin, palm wine, and other native luxuries. Kanky is the native bread, made from Indian corn, or cassada, ground down, by rubbing between stones into a meal, and then made into the consistency of boiled ground rice by mixing with water. It is very insiped food, but the people live very much upon it with a little fish fried in palm oil, roast plantains or ground nut soup. They do not eat often, only once or twice a day, the principal meal being about sunset.

I witnessed a native funeral procession. The corpse was in a wooden coffin covered with a coloured cloth, and carried on men's shoulders. The followers sang a lively kind of chant, and clapped their hands continually. Men ran beside the procession firing guns. Both men and women were present. I was informed that after being carried all round the town in this manner, the body would be buried under the house the person had lived in when alive, which would then be deserted for a time. It is this habit of burying the dead within the town, together with the utter regardlessness of sanitary law, that makes Elmina so unhealthy, and I am not at all surprised that the first detachment of marines sent there suffered so much. The water also is very bad. Within the fort is a well of excellent water, but that is kept for the use of the garrison. What the natives drink is taken from the ditch of the fort, into which drains much of the filth I have before alluded to. Rum and gin of the worst description are plentiful and cheap, and do not tend to improve the health of either natives or Europeans careless enough to drink such stuff.

Domestic slavery exists everywhere on the Gold Coast. This I was not surprised at, but I was very much so to find that the Court presided over by our British judge took cognisance of the institution, and could direct a reluctant slave to return to his master and be obedient to him! At the same time, if a slave could prove cruelty against his master, he was at once set free ; the inevitable result of such a course would be that the man would sell himself again as soon as he could find a purchaser. Slave holders are obliged to support their property in sickness or old age, and to pay them a proportion of their earnings, and it is a point of honour not to sell them off the land they belong to. It is the slaveowners who appear to me the most anxious to abolish slavery ; the slaves do less, and live better, than they will as free men. A story is told of a newly arrived gentleman offering slaves freedom—or rather telling them that as Queen Victoria's subjects they were free. They seemed very rejoiced at this at first, until they came to ask " what Queen Victoria was going to give them ?" expecting something very good from so rich a sovereign, when their countenance fell, as they learnt what freedom meant.

Certainly, our laws should not recognize the

property of man in man in any country, but least of all in Africa, where our whole policy has been devoted to the abolition of the slave trade, and our action on the Gold Coast is very unintelligible to foreigners.

We sailed from Elmina on the 29th May, and on the morning of the 31st were off Assini, where the French Protectorate joins ours on its western frontier. The French had removed their officials from here and Grand Bassam during the last few days, the nature of the country making it difficult to enforce obedience to law among the native tribes. Thus, Danes, Dutch, and French have given up their Protectorates on this coast, and the British alone are left to carry on this most unsatisfactory of all modes of government. It is to be hoped that after the present war is concluded, the Gold Coast will be declared British territory and governed after the Indian fashion; or, that a Consulate with local courts of equity will be established, and the country given over to native government, as is the case in the oil rivers.

The little difficulty which caused the French to leave was, that a trading hulk had been robbed by the natives; the government demanded of the native chief the value of the goods taken. The chief promised to pay, but after many months, had only paid a small portion of the money. The French Admiral then blockaded the coast. This had not the least effect on the natives who could afford to wait, they got their more pressing needs supplied from Appolonia in our protectorate, so the French withdrew entirely, although I believe they still say they protect Grand Bassam and Assini.

There was a very heavy surf preventing all communication with the shore whilst we were off the factories, except with great risk of being capsized. A surf boat did reach us with a letter but she was several times capsized. The river Assini is of considerable size, and, inside its bar, affords extensive and safe inland communication ; a small steamer occasionally plies upon it and the lagoons in connection with it for trading purposes. The coast was low, and beach sandy, with mangrove trees close behind it, bespeaking unhealthy swamps. The factories appeared commodious, and trade was recommencing after the blockade ; casks of palm oil were to be seen on the beach awaiting the arrival of the mail steamer.

No chance appearing of the swell going down I steamed away for Cape Palmas. We encountered a current against us at the rate of three miles an hour. Whilst at Cape Coast the Governor told me a bottle had been sent in from Appolonia that was thrown overboard from H.M.S. *Druid* at sea, 600 miles to the westward, a month previously, on her voyage to the Cape. So it had travelled at an average rate of 20 miles a day to the east.

As we neared Cape Palmas the land rose higher again, was covered with trees, and we could see some mountains in the interior. This is a very rainy part of the world, but the season was at its close, and we only came in for an occasional shower.

Harper, as the town is called, looks well from the sea, with its two or three church spires among the trees, and shingled frame houses of two stories surrounded by gardens. It is the second town of Liberia, the capital being Monrovia, some distance to the north. It is said to contain 2,000 or 3,000 inhabitants, has three or four churches, an academy, a hospital, an orphan asylum, and a light-house. The latter is more an ornament than of use, the Republic not being able to afford funds to light it up. The harbour affords shelter to vessels of light draught, and we had a few days relief from constant rolling whilst we staid here.

Liberia was purchased by the Americans from the native chiefs about 30 years ago, as a place to colonize with emancipated slaves from the States, and the government was as soon as possible given into the negroes' own hands. The Americans were too wise to saddle themselves with a Liberian Protectorate.

Colonists still arrive from the States, sent over by a society which pays their passage, and allows them subsistence money during the first six months they are in Africa. The Liberian Government gives them a grant of land, and as it brings forth abundantly, and has neither too few nor too many trees, it is the settler's own fault if he does not prosper. And I suppose the people may be called prosperous—not according to English notions : but for negroes and ex-slaves certainly so. If they would not ape white-man's ways and be so insufferably conceited, they would be all the better.

The gentleman who came off to pay me an official visit of welcome, spoke of the natives, who had not had the honour of coming from America, as " heathen," although these people I found had quite as good reason to call themselves Christians as my friend had. On another occasion one of our officers, when on shore, was accosted by a negro of the ordinary coast type, as " Doctor." He replied, " I am not the doctor, you sabbe ; that man in the white hat, he doctor."

" Sir," replied the negro, " I don't understand your language, we are an educated people here, and are not accustomed to use the word sabbe."

" Oh !" said the innocent offender, " I am very sorry, I did'nt intend to hurt your feelings !"

" I accept your apology," said Sambo gravely, " and attribute your speech to your ignorance; good day, sah !"

Every person I met had a title. I was introduced to Colonel Cooper, of the 4th Liberian regiment, who informed me their army never did any fighting but had regular quarterly musters and annual reviews.

Governor Gibson I thought an intelligent man. He evidently does not live entirely on his official income, as he did us the honour to supply us with fresh beef and vegetables, at a very fair price. Coin of the realm was scarce; the only Liberian money I saw was paper; the storekeepers were delighted to see our metallic currency.

The houses were nearly all built of wood; the Episcopal Church was of brick and had a spire; inside it was whitewashed; over the communion table, and the windows, some texts were written in black paint, which had evidently been put on with one of the artists fingers!

I found one white lady, as the matron of the Orphan Asylum, but she was the only white person in the place. She was the widow of a missionary who died at Harper a few years previously.

A few wheeled vehicles were seen now and then drawn by oxen or donkeys, and there was a passable road or two out of the town. The gardens were tidy, and there was a good deal of live stock. Corn, coffee, and rice are grown by the farmers. The "heathen" make very good boatmen and sailors.

The weather was cool during our stay, a pleasant south wind blowing, locally termed the "salt" wind, as it bore some of the ocean salt on its breeze, which deposited itself on plants, etc.

Although Harper stands on high ground I think it cannot be healthy, owing to the damp, from the great quantity of rain, which penetrates everything; but I was told that although there was a medical practitioner in the place, he could not live by his profession, and was forced to work a farm. This might have been from lack of fees and not from lack of practice. As our doctor was much asked for, I think this must be the case.

CHAPTER III.

THE object which brought me to Palmas was to enquire into the "coast labour traffic," and this is one of the principal markets for labourers. All vessels trading on the coast, and most factories, employ labourers, boatmen, &c., (under the generic name of Kroomen,) from Sierra Leone, Monrovia, or Palmas. These men ship for sailors, and work by the voyage, at a rate of 10d. or 1s. a day, but for factory work, for a period of a year or two, for 15s. a month and rations. When factors require them they either send a "book," or note, to the purser of the outward bound steamer to bring them down so many Kroomen; or they send a head Krooman up to select the men they want. The factor pays 30s. passage money for the Kroomen, and 6d. a day for provisions. But other Kroomen come on board beside those required for the ship, or going "to order." These men go down the coast on speculation. If they find a factor wanting hands, they hire themselves to him if he pays their passage, but as the steamer turns round to come homewards, the officers of the steamers sooner than lose the passage money altogether, hire them out on the best terms they can.

It appeared to me that there was an opening here for a slave trade to spring up in a new form unless it was watched.

At Fernando Po, my attention was first drawn to the matter, by two Palmas lads complaining to me that they had been landed six months previously against their will, and that they had ever since been virtually slaves, obliged to work without receiving anything but food and a little cloth to cover themselves. Taking their statement for what it was worth, I made further enquiries, and was told that the lads that came down looking for chance employment were sometimes given to the native chiefs in the oil rivers. Then, on boarding a mail steamer at Cape Coast, we found more than one hundred natives on board who were neither on the ships muster roll nor passenger list, and Lieutenant Sperling of the *Coquette*, found one with still more on board. The Administrator of the Gold Coast also informed me that the traffic was irregular and required looking into.

I received a letter from Mr. Gibson, shortly after my arrival at Palmas, informing me that he had heard of the object of my visit, and expressing his satisfaction that some notice was at last taken of the labour traffic carried on by British steamers, and offering to give me every information. But I found that the Governor had only to complain of the ill usage Kroomen passengers received on board the steamers.

E 2

He admitted that there was no such thing as kidnapping, and that there were generally more men ready to go down the coast than the steamers would take, and that most of them returned with a fair amount of money, or money's worth, in their possession. Still, he said, the local chiefs had complained to him that not a few of their people were never heard of again.

Speaking to the captain of one of the steamers about the reason for not entering Kroomen on the passenger list, he said, they were so apt to be stolen or desert, that it would be impossible to keep a correct list.

I asked Mr. Gibson to mention the particular ill-treatment he had heard Kroomen complain of. He mentioned a circumstance that had lately occurred. A steamer called off the port to discharge her Kroomen passengers; there was no cargo for her and she did not wish to stop, and as the canoes were some time coming off, the Kroomen with their baggage were forced overboard to swim to them, so as not to detain the steamer. He mentioned bad food, and other matters; but I must say, I have never heard complaints elsewhere on this subject, or from the Kroomen themselves, but our Kroomen whom I used as interpreters, were Sierra Leone men, and could not often understand Palmas men.

I made my report to our Government through Commodore Commerell, and the trade will be watched.

There is no doubt it is a great blessing to our coast trade to be able to employ these men, and if properly carried on, the Kroomen are equally benefitted.

We returned to Cape Coast on the 10th June. On landing I met the funeral of Mr. Bate, a Wesleyan missionary, who had died from an attack of dysentery that morning. The following was very large of men and women. The " trowser" men wore black frock coats, and white, or shiny black hats, and the " petticoat" ladies, nice black dresses and bonnets ; the " clouty" men and women, who were many, looked none the less respectful and respectable. The rear of the procession was brought up by a chief's umbrella, and stick bearers.

The cemetery is not as nicely kept as might be expected, and I heard a complaint that the natives are given to mutilate head stones from a mere spirit of mischief.

We did not stay at Cape Coast, but sailed immediately for Lagos, calling at intermediate ports. At Jellah Coffee we again replenished our live stock. Then we passed alongshore looking in at Porto Seguro, Great Popo, Whydah and Appi, at all of which places we found sailing vessels loading or discharging cargo. They were chiefly French. The pea-nut is taken to Marseilles by these vessels to produce the best " olive oil !" At Popo a large English barque had been wrecked in a gale that had occurred a few weeks previously. A

gale of wind is a very rare event in the Bights, and
vessels are induced to anchor too close to the shore for
safety, to facilitate loading operations. The natives
had plundered this wreck of her cargo and materials,
considering it as a godsend, and, we were told, asked
also for a " Dash" for saving the crew ! The merchant
to whom the cargo belonged was too wise to ask for a
man-of-war to punish the natives in the usual manner
for this outrage, contenting himself with a much more
profitable and satisfactory manner of recouping his
loss in the ordinary course of business.

The landing is very bad all along this coast, and
must be done at all times in the usual surf boat. The
coast is low, and immediately within the strip of sand
forming the sea shore are large lagoons of shallow
water, which render it a most unhealthy place for
Europeans to live in. From Accra on the Gold Coast,
until the Cameroon mountains are reached, this is so, a
distance of more than 500 miles. This may be called
the country of the Delta of the Niger, for there is a
probability that all the lagoons and rivers that enter
the sea within these limits are connected with that
great river.

On the 16th June we anchored off Lagos bar.
There were about 20 merchant vessels in the roads, but
we were told trade was very dull, owing to a tribe in
the interior having become hostile to us, and they had
established a kind of internal blockade, locally termed

"Stopping the roads." Captain Glover, R.N., who had ably administered the government of this settlement for many years, had left for England on the previous day, and Mr. Hennessy was in Lagos.

The *Torch* drew too much water to cross the bar ; so Lieutenant Larcom was good enough to come out in H.M.S. *Pioneer*, which was, on our arrival, at anchor off the town, to take me in. The bar has a frightful appearance, as it is approached. It is a mass of foaming breakers, stretching apparently from one side of Lagos river to the other, at least three miles. But there are passages through it by which skilled pilots can take small vessels in and out, but the channels are constantly changing. Once inside the bar, a fine expanse of smooth water is reached with a deep channel. If the bar could be deepened by artificial means this would become one of the finest harbours on the coast.

The late season had been very unhealthy, and there were so few white persons left in Lagos, that Captain Glover had been obliged to ask Lieutenant Larcom temporarily to perform the duties of Colonial Secretary and Treasurer. To show how trade had been affected by the blockade I have spoken of, and by the prohibition of Governor Glover to export guns or powder to the native tribes who had "stopped the roads," Mr. Larcom told me that he found three shillings and sixpence in the Colonial chest when he took office, and on his resignation a fortnight afterwards it contained 14s. 9d !

The annual revenue of the settlement had, I was informed, once reached to nearly £40,000.

I remembered Lagos as a native town surrounded by mangrove swamp, and the head quarters of the slave trade in the Bight of Benin. This, in 1850. I was truly astonished to find it what it is. It is situated on an island, very low of course, but the mangrove has been cleared a long way back, and it is no longer a swamp. As we steamed towards Government house in the *Pioneer* we passed several handsome villa residences, and the grand stand of a race course !

We found the Governor and chief officials had gone to breakfast with King Docemo, whose family ruled in Lagos before it fell into our hands, and who receives an annual pension from the Colonial chest. I believe he performs some judicial functions in native disputes. His breakfast I heard pronounced a success; he adopted as nearly as he could the European style of giving it, but he could not make European cooks or waiters out of native materials.

Government house is neither the most imposing nor commodious in the place, and not to be compared to that at Cape Coast in this matter, showing that past Governors had not paid so much attention to their own comforts as to the improvement of the settlement. The town is certainly a great and standing credit to them. The Marina, facing the water, is more than a mile long. A well kept road shaded by trees goes along its whole extent; wooden wharves, alongside which ships were laying, project from it into the sea, and on the land side, separated by neat gardens from the road, were stucco houses of two or three stories, with green verandahs round them. The shops and stores were well stocked, and the market well supplied. The native town is separated from the more fashionable quarter where Europeans reside, and contains about 30,000 inhabitants.

The officials and merchants of Lagos are famed for their hospitality, and we enjoyed our short visit to them. There was again a great want, although not an entire absence of ladies' society, but Lagos climate is a bad one,—much worse than Cape Coast.

I had the pleasure of making the acquaintance of Mrs. Davis, formerly Miss Bonneta Forbes, a god-daughter of her Majesty, and whom she had had educated in England. She had been taken out of a captured slaver by Captain Forbes and taken to England, or brought from Dahomy by him after his visit to the king,—I forget which. She bears on her cheek the marks made on Dahoman slaves. Captain Davis, her husband, appears a prosperous merchant, and their house is furnished with much taste. He, also, is an African native.

Bishop Crowther is well known in this country. At home he is a simple, pleasant, and obliging gentleman. He was enthusiastic about the capabilities of the Niger country, and the capacity of that noble river for a large trade.   He spoke in very high terms of the increasing friendliness of the river tribes, and was very sanguine about the progress of missionary enterprise in that region.   He told how, in a recent overland journey he had made from a place on the Niger to Lagos, his party received presents from the native chiefs valued at no less than £400.   Missionaries connected with different Protestant societies are established at Lagos, and there are several churches. A very large Episcopal church was in course of con-struction, and I visited a pretty one in which the Bishop officiated, beside which the old building, built after the native fashion, is still used.

Horses thrive very well at Lagos, and some neat traps are to be met driving about its streets.   Altogether, Lagos has a more civilized air about it than any town we visited, between Dâkar and St. Pauls de Loando.

Mr. Porter, the agent for Messrs. Banner Brothers, informed me that he had resided for a considerable time in the large native town of Abbeokuta, whose walls are seventeen miles in circumference.   Abbeokuta is not far from Lagos, inland, and in a healthier climate. Day by day its demands for European goods are increasing, and it is likely to become a good English customer, when paths are open, and our policy better understood.

There are one or two out stations of importance in

the Lagos settlement of which Badagry to the west is
the chief, and the trade prospects of the settlement are
so good, if peace can be established on its borders, that
it is likely to go on increasing in wealth and political
importance and to become the Liverpool of the Coast.

On the 19th we sailed for Old Calabar. We had
occasional heavy showers, but not every day, and
seldom of any length. Average maximum of thermometer 86°. It was difficult to recognise one mouth
of the Niger from another, they are all so much
alike between the Benin and the Nun. The shore is
covered with mangrove trees ; occasionally, some of
another species intrude themselves, and an umbrella
tree may be seen rising above the rest at long intervals,
as the only variety to the scene on the most monotonous
coast man ever looked upon. After passing Cape
Formosa the mud deposited by the rivers forms shoals
miles out to seaward, rendering it unsafe for ships to
approach too close to the land.

We fell in with H.M.S. *Druid* off the Bonny, and
received orders from Captain Nelson to visit Gaboon
and other ports, and to return to Cape Coast.

On the 24th June we anchored off the Old Calabar
river, the rain falling in torrents. The weather did
not clear until the afternoon of the 25th, when we
could make out the marks for entering the river.
" Tom Shot's breakers" are eight miles from the
entrance, and within them are many dangers to navi-

gation, and a strong tide. A few buoys have been put down by the merchants interested in the trade of the river to mark the turning points, but the sounding lead is the great guide. Curiously, there is hard bottom on one side of the channel and soft bottom on the other; so, if the soundings decrease, you know at once on which side of deep water you are. The river is several miles wide for the first 40 miles, but it then narrows to a considerable stream not less than a mile across until Duke town is reached. We did not arrive there that night, the tide not suiting; but early on the 26th we went up with the flood tide at a great pace. We only remained a few hours whilst I got through some business with Consul Livingstone, who was residing at the Scotch Missionary Station. This is built on some high ground overlooking the river. The site is a lovely one and the premises well kept. The house is as comfortable as could be wished. I cannot say much for the external beauty of the church, which has a round roof of galvanized iron like a railway goods depôt. Mr. Livingstone showed me some great natural curiosities—fish with eyelids. They were about four inches long, of a light colour, and capable of giving a palpable electric shock—they were alive, and swimming about in a basin.

The merchants resided on board large hulks, roofed over with galvanized iron, moored in the river. Trade —palm oil—appeared very brisk; two steamers were loading, and the river looked busy with large canoes and cargo boats.

We left again before noon at high water, and reached Fernando Po during the night. There we coaled, and took the *Pioneer* in tow as far as Cape Lopez. She then went on to the Congo and we entered the Gaboon.

Unlike the Congo, this magnificent river has numerous dangers at its entrance, and the tide runs in almost as fast as it runs out. In the Congo the flood tide, although there is an equal rise as at Gaboon, seldom even checks the force of the surface current.

The French settlement is on the north bank of the river, and consists of a small dockyard with storehouses and coal sheds, barracks, hospital, church, schools, and official residences. Stores and private residences are scattered about, but they are few and of no great pretension.

We anchored on the 29th June. The Acting-Governor was the Captain of the receiving hulk, the Admiral commanding on the station not having arrived from France. He is ex-officio Governor of Gaboon and the protectorate of Grand Bassam. Gaboon is situated a few miles north of the equator. The climate is one of the pleasantest on the coast, but the commander of the *Pygmée* informed me that the river was very unhealthy as it was ascended. Where the settlement is, the land rises considerably, and there are no mangroves near it, and the inhabitants get the full benefit of a delicious sea breeze every afternoon. The river is entered by a deep channel, but it becomes too shoal for vessels of more than a very light draught at a distance of 25 miles from its entrance. Small steamers can navigate its numerous branches, some of them for at least 150 miles. It is not yet thoroughly surveyed, and the trade of the river is quite in its infancy.

There are two large and interesting missionary establishments. The French one, presided over by a Bishop, receives support from government. The children educated here are taught to cultivate the various agricultural products that flourish in the country. They are also taught how to prepare these articles for market. The gardens are very extensive, well kept, and well stocked. Among other things, I was shown coffee, cocoa, palm of varieties, mango, bread fruit, banana, orange, and lime trees ; sugar canes and grape vines of several varieties, pine apples, papaws, and cotton bushes, all flourishing. Rice is cultivated on a strip of land near the river. Vegetables grow remarkably well, and fine cabbages, lettuce, celery, beetroot, turnips, carrots, onions, and marrows were shown. Potatoes have been grown but do not do well. The sweet potato there is no difficulty about. The gardens are artificially irrigated in the dry season, but there is not much trouble in doing this where labour is so cheap, and these gardens prove what the soil is capable of.

There were 150 boys in the schools, and the Sisters of Mercy educated a number of girls at another place. Some of the boys are taught trades, such as blacksmiths, carpenters, and coopers; how to manage cattle and rear poultry, and how to use machines for sugar making and extracting oil from cocoa nuts and seeds. They are also educated in the French and native (M'Pongwe) languages, and taught mathematics if required. The more intelligent lads are sent to Senegal or France to be educated for the priesthood. The church is provided with an organ, stained glass windows, and is well appointed.

The other missionary station is that belonging to the American Board of Missions and situated two miles further up the river at Glass town. It is a beautiful spot, on ground much above the river, with a magnificent view. The Rev. Mr. Bushnell is at its head, and his wife has resided here with him for many years; other American ladies were also at the station. The houses, schoolrooms, stores, and church were all one storied buildings, thatched with palm leaves and surrounded by shady verandahs. The gravel walks were lined with trimmed hedges, the gardens bright with oleanders and roses; and the fields in which the cows were grazing had quite a homely look. Mrs. Bushnell succeeded in making butter, solid butter, from her cream, and this on the equator! The children educated here were also taught to be useful, and to produce from

the soil its wonderful latent wealth. Of course religious and secular knowledge was taught in the schools,
and Mr. Bushnell stated that many of the lads taught
there were doing well in America and Africa. It is an
unfortunate fact, though, that educated natives find a
better opening for their abilities out of Africa than in
it!

We enjoyed some pleasant walks during our stay,
the paths being hard, and trees shady. The native
female dress was remarkable. The cloths were of
brighter colour than usual and more ample. The hair
was done into still more fantastical shapes than on the
Gold Coast, and the bracelets of large beads reached
sometimes to the elbows, and leglets from the ankle to
the knee. Ivory ornaments seemed the fashion also
for men and women. I believe each locality has its
own pattern of bead, and certain families on the South
Coast keep to one pattern cloth.

As this is the Gorilla country, I expected to hear
something of the animal. None of the French officers
had ever seen one alive, although one officer had been
nearly three years on the station and many months in
the interior. Mr. Bushnell during a residence of more
than 25 years had seen two young ones, dead. They
are evidently not common. There are many leopards
in the country, and they are nuisances to stock-keepers.
I saw traps for taking them—strongly built wooden
houses, closed by a heavy door, by the animal touching

a spring when it enters. A kid or a pig is used as a bait. It is put alive into an inner chamber, fenced by iron railings from the outer. Large nails were driven into the sides of the trap I saw, and into the roof, to prevent the animal jumping against the cage when it finds itself entrapped, and so forcing its way out.

I saw the horns of some large antelopes that had been shot close to, and was told that there was feathered game to be had under the usual difficulties. Elephants did not come nearer than the Chrystal Mountains. A priest of the mission who had resided there for some time told me they were very numerous. It is about 50 miles from the settlement, and a great part of the journey can be made by water.

The M'Pongwe language is one of the most perfect on the West African Coast. Mr. Bushnell and the French priests have reduced it to writing and published a grammar for school use, and translated portions of the Bible and other books into it, but it appeared to me very cumbersome.

In the race between the French and English languages in this district, I think the English will win, for nearly all the trade is carried on by our merchants. Palm oil, dye and hard woods, and India rubber, are the exports; the imports as usual—guns, powder, cloth, rum, gin, and trash.

I left Gaboon on the 6th July and paid another visit to Corisco. It was a busy time with the traders,

F

the rains inland having ceased, and the Bushmen were bringing India rubber, wax, ivory, and dye woods to market. I went on board a hulk at the entrance of the Muni, the fore part was crowded with produce being prepared for shipment to Europe, and India rubber and oil are not cleanly looking things; but the after part of the ship was comfortably and cooly furnished, and the usual hospitable reception ready from its occupiers. They reported trade improving and natives less troublesome. The natives look to be an inferior race. The canoes with which they bring down produce from the interior are hollowed out of very large trees, some of astonishing size. I saw some like them at Gaboon which had been captured formerly by French men-of-war, taking slaves to the island of St. Thomas, and I was informed had sixty men in each.

Our stay was very short. As we proceeded out of the bay, we sent a boat to examine the wreck of the *Macgregor Laird*, whose funnel alone was to be seen above water. While the boat was pulling round the wreck, a cask came suddenly to the surface. It was branded "Pale Ale, Bass and Co., Burton-on-Trent!" It was brought on board as a prize, and its contents directed to be issued to the men, the ownership of the cask being very doubtful. But alas for anticipated pleasure! The contents were very foul smelling and apparently bilge water!

On the 8th we arrived at Fernando Po. Coaling is

never a pleasant operation, but here least of all. The heat was the greatest we ever experienced on the coast, 94° in the shade, and coal dust penetrated everywhere. Going on shore to escape being choked by it, I found the heat even greater, and the numerous insects almost as annoying as the coal dust. It was astonishing to see the great weights of coal the Kroomen will carry at a time. I saw one of our men, Jack Smart, carry two bags, or 400-lbs, on his head at one time from the shed to the boat, a distance of 70 yards. These Kroomen are fine fellows for coast work. They are not exactly sailors, although some of them learn to be, but good boatmen, and useful labourers, accustomed to the sea. On board a man-of war they wear the usual seamen's uniform, and it is their pride to keep their kits in first-rate order. They live on the upper deck by themselves, and have a head Krooman as a petty officer over them. They require very little punishment, are quite amenable to discipline, and work hard. Among themselves they speak their own language, but they understand orders given to them in English. Some speak excellent English. They are entered on a ship's books when they first join the service by some English name, which they keep while they remain. Among ours were Tom Dollar, Tom Peter, Sodawater, Black Will, and Bottle o' Beer, and similar names. We carried twelve of these men,—some large ships have thirty.

They are seldom drilled to the guns or the use of ·

F 2

small arms, but when they are they become expert, and
for Africans are passing brave. They are very clever
canoemen and capital swimmers. The canoe they use
is a light shapely one for two or four paddlers, who
have to squat on their knees in a most uncomfortable
position to paddle; they can bring these canoes off
shore through a heavy surf on their own coast, which
is a little south of Sierra Leone. They have some
curious fashions of their own,—among others, it is considered rather well bred to have nine toes, and they
will sometimes injure one of the little ones on purpose
to have it amputated. They will worry the doctor
also to pull their front teeth out. They are fond of
taking medicine, but have no faith in its efficacy unless
there is plenty of it, and it is very nasty.

CHAPTER IV.

THE passage from Fernando Po to Cape Coast was completely yachting work in a smooth sea, light breeze, and cool atmosphere. The thermometer dropped 15° on clearing the island, and during the mornings and evenings we had most enjoyable weather. Our two or three feverish cases recovered, and a plague of boils that had set in, subsided.

We anchored at Cape Coast on the 17th July. The *Druid* was here, and about to proceed to Elmina. The murderers of Mr. Joorst had been convicted and sentenced to be hung. Preparations were being made to put the sentence into execution, and a disturbance was anticipated. On shore, at Cape Coast, I heard doubts of their guilt expressed. It was thought that the native King, supposing himself bound to give up some of his people to our Governor, as the murderers, had given up these men on the assurance that he had also power enough to get their sentence commuted to a fine, which he would pay. There is no doubt that he exerted all his power with Mr. Hennessy to get their sentence commuted to imprisonment or fine, and that he said that was the plan always followed by the Dutch. But Mr. Hennessy thought it necessary to impress the native mind at once with the British horror of the crime of assassination, and would not hold out the least hope of commuting the Judge's sentence. It is even thought by many that the King himself was the instigator of the murder. He is not at all contented with the transfer to our " protection," and is angry with the Dutch for leaving him. On the 22nd, at 8 a.m., the men were hung from a gallows erected on the walls of Fort St. George facing the town. To the last moment the people could not believe the sentence would be carried out, even the prisoners themselves could not be brought to think their King so powerless, having promised to rescue them. However, to prepare for the worst, they swallowed as much gold dust as their friends would bring them, and it was no inconsiderable quantity ! This sure way of taking their property to the grave is usual with those about to die, and if it cannot be done, money, clothes, arms and food are buried with the body. I am not quite sure of the Fantee belief in a future life, but it exists to some degree, and little sheds are found near every house where food and water are regularly placed for the departed ones to refresh themselves, when they pay nightly visits to their old homes.

The executions passed off quietly, a native prisoner in the fort, acting as Jack Ketch ; not a person appeared in the streets. The bodies were afterwards buried in the Castle yard. There is no doubt that the Elmina people were much subdued after this event.

The following story I relate with great diffidence, not being learned in natural history, and having my eyes and the eyes of those who were present on the occasion alone to trust to, to guide me in describing what we witnessed. Captain the Hon. M. H. Nelson, H.M.S. *Druid*, and Commander Prescott Stephens, H.M.S. *Bittern*, were about to leave the *Torch*, on the evening of the 26th July, then at anchor off Cape Coast, to return to the *Druid* which was off Elmina, when our attention was drawn to a great commotion in the water at about half-a-mile from the ship, and presently a large eel-shaped fish, with dark back and white belly, put its head, or what appeared to be its head, about 20 or 30 feet into the air, and came down with a great thwack on the water twice, when a whale of great size, bottle nose, length not less than 60 feet, sprang into the air, coming down with a splash that may be imagined. This was repeated two or three times, the whale ultimately going away to sea. I was told afterwards the other fish was a 'thresher.' It might have been its tail and not its head we saw, for its movements were too rapid, and the splashing of the water too great to see distinctly. It appeared to us, in size round, about twice that of a man's body. The depth of water in which this took place was about 10 fathoms.

Lieutenant Jeffreys and the officers of the *Torch* all witnessed, and all were equally surprised at the incident. I saw the same thing again a few days afterwards near Bootry, also in shoal water, but much less of the thresher appeared above water, and the whale's jump was much higher and more frequent. I have seen whales jumping in this way also off the River Congo.

On the 28th July, we embarked a detachment of the 2nd West India Regiment and some Fantee police for Accra, a slight diffculty having arisen between two neighbouring tribes. We arrived next morning. The landing is worse than Cape Coast; on the open beach, with the Atlantic swell breaking on it, of course a surf boat had to be used. The canoe men sing the same kind of song; the refrain "Dash me, dollar!" was duly attended to by me, on going ashore, lest I should get a wet jacket.

The town of Accra is much more scattered than that at Cape Coast; it is built on top of a red cliff, some 60 feet high, over-looking the sea. The country around has a parched appearance; there are few trees and few gardens. Formerly there were three Accras, British and Dutch close together, and Danish two miles east. Danish Accra is called also Christiansborg. The Dutch and Danes having left, Christiansborg is nearly deserted, and the other two towns have become one.

Officials were scarce at Accra as they appeared to

me always to be on the Gold Coast, and I found it
difficult to find anyone to transact business with.
Trade in palm oil seemed brisk, but not equal to Cape
Coast. I met Mr. Freeman, a coloured gentleman, who
had been for some years established as a missionary at
Coomassie, and who spoke well of the Ashantees.
Although the popular language at Accra differs from
Cape Coast, the customs and dress appeared the same.
A great many of the people are Christians. They
belong to the Wesleyan body.

On a tombstone at Accra is recorded that 300
soldiers, in whose memory it is erected, died there of
fever in three days! I think there must be some mis-
take in figures about this, for the place is considered
healthy.

The fort is a very small place, used as a prison for
natives. It is not a pleasant place to be confined in.
I was told most of the prisoners there were in for debt.
The creditors have to pay 6d. a day for their keep, or
it would be more full than it is, for all Africans have a
delight in running into debt, without an idea of how
they are to pay. However none of the prisons that I
have seen in the forts on the Gold Coast, would bear
inspection by our prison authorities or sanitary commissioners; the only thing I can say is, from what I
have heard and seen, things used to be worse, especially
with the Dutch. At Bootry I crawled into a damp
cell, with just room enough to squat down in, without

window—it was underground—or light of any kind,
or air except what came through the chinks in the door
which led into another room; this cell had been a
prison to confine offenders of serious crimes in in the
time of Dutch protection.   At Appolonia, built by the
British, the prison was lighted and ventilated by a hole
two feet in diameter in the roof.   This fort has not
been used by us for several years, and the Dutch may
have altered it.   I have seen prisoners grinning through
iron gratings at Elmina and at Axim from very unpleasant looking quarters.

On the 30th we returned to Elmina.   Here I received a commission from the Acting-Administrator to
proceed to the Western frontier, in conjunction with
the civil commandant at Axim, to endeavour to open
the road for traffic between Assini and Axim, at present
stopped by tribal wars, and to endeavour to establish
peace in the district.   Captain Nelson having given his
permission that I should perform this duty for the
colony, and having placed the *Torch* at the Administrator's service for a short period, we proceeded on our
mission on the 1st August.   We took with us a large
surf boat and crew of Elmina men for the purpose of
landing through the bad surf.   Mr. Molenaar, a half-
caste gentleman of Dutch extraction, accompanied us
as interpreter. He is a very clever linguist, and is
acquainted with the politics and customs of the
Western tribes. He was also entrusted with the

presents to be given to the chiefs as "Dash," as he knew what would be most acceptable, and the proper amount to be given to each.

We also took Mr. Hughes as passenger to Dix Cove, of which place he had been appointed Civil Comman-dant. We reached Dix Cove that afternoon. It is a small native town overlooked by an old fort, from the walls of which was displayed the Union Jack. There were two large slated houses, before which also the Union Jack was flying. I found they belonged to a native, who had grown very rich in the palm oil trade, and who was intensely loyal to the British, and equally inveterate against the Dutch. He pointed with pride to some marks of shot holes in his houses, which had been made by his neighbours in the fort, when it had been in Dutch occupation.

It is necessary before going further to say a few words in explanation of the political position of this country.

Prior to 1868 all European nations had abandoned the forts they had established on the Gold Coast, to protect their trade and the tribes they traded with, except the British and Dutch. Their forts almost alternated with one another. Thus Appolonia was British; Axim, Dutch; Dix Cove, British; Bootry, Dutch; and so on. This system was found to work badly for both governments and led to many complica-tions. In 1868 an arrangement was made, whereby all

forts belonging to the Dutch on the Gold Coast, eastward of Cape Coast, were transferred to the British;
and all forts belonging to the British, westward, were
transferred to the Dutch. The natives who were " protected" do not seem to have had much voice in the
matter, and, indeed, I do not think their wishes are ever
consulted. The transfer created much discontent among
the tribes who changed masters; but in our newly
acquired districts, after a little while, the people became
fairly contented. It was otherwise with the Dutch.
Commendah flatly refused to receive their flag, and was
knocked to pieces by the guns of a man-of-war for so
doing; and Dix Cove received a good dose of round
and grape from the fort, to bring it to a proper sense of
its duty.

Dutch officers were allowed to supplement the small
official salaries they received by trading, and as they
used the forts as their storehouses, and paid no duty on
imports, they drove all competitors out of the market;
and the import duties received to pay the expenses of
the government were so small as to be only nominal.
This was unsatisfactory to two parties: the Dutch
government, who found the settlement such an un-
profitable concern as ultimately to make it necessary to
abandon it, and the old traders, English and native, who
found themselves ruined by the Dutch official trader.

Besides, the tribes under different protectorates had
always been jealous of each other. Wars between

neighbouring towns were frequent, and now Dutch
Commandants came to govern and to judge all the
western tribes, of course their old friends expected
favour, and the former aliens disfavour at their hands ;
and they received it.

Now, in 1872, the Dutch had again transferred the
Western district to the British: there was joy at the
former British stations, such as Dix Cove, but mourning
and anxiety at the old Dutch stations, as at Bootry and
Axim. The Administrator even thought that forcible
resistance might be made to our authority at Bootry,
so that I was directed to be present, to give support to
the Commandant of Dix Cove, when he hoisted our
flag on Bootry fort.

Bootry is only a few miles from Dix Cove, and like
the latter a small native trading village overlooked by
an old fort. Our government did not intend to garrison
the fort, or place a Commandant in the town, it was to
be "protected" from Dix Cove. We proceeded to it
next morning with Mr. Hughes and Doctor Goldsbury,
who had been Acting-Commandant before Mr. Hughes
arrival. Bootry is a pretty spot, with a better landing
place than usual. White men had been rarely seen,
and we were objects of curiosity. We met Captain
Hoare, Messrs. Swanzy's agent, trading here, and he
most kindly promised to join our expedition. He
knew the western chiefs well.

The flag was hoisted at Bootry fort without any
disturbance, or expression of feeling in any way.

A salute of 21 guns was fired from the fort. I was present, but when I saw the way the gunners loaded the guns, I thought it better to take a walk. The King had lent Mr. Hughes some natives to do the honour to our flag. Their procedure was to take a small barrel of gun-powder under their arm and knock the head in; then tilting the mouths of the guns upwards, to pour into them as much powder as they thought would make a good noise, on top of which they rammed a wad of grass: another man primed with a horn and "devil," made of damp powder, a third fired with a lighted stick which he swung about to keep it burning.

Barrels of spare powder were kept in the rear of the guns!

The salute ended without accident; and I was informed the native King had received our flag, and our presents. He and his chiefs had been received in in the "palavar" hall of the fort, and duly admonished of their duty of loyalty to their new protectors.

I found Doctor Goldsbury busy in the town vaccinating adults and children. He told me it had become a Fantee fashion to be vaccinated and to be able to show the marks on the arm, so that the demand for his services was extreme. Small-pox creates great ravages among the natives, but since the vaccination had become fashionable its effects had been palpably lessened.

We returned to Dix Cove the same afternoon.

Mr. Hughes' and Mr Goldsbury's quarters were very wretched. The fort was in bad repair and very damp, and a famous preserve of centipedes and resort of snakes, etc. The furniture of it sold to us by the Dutch was mere rubbish. I believe we paid about the eighth part of their valuation for it. The two gentlemen I have named are the only white inhabitants. The fort is garrisoned by a Sergeant's party of the 2nd West. Doctor Goldsbury had, previous to Mr. Hughes' arrival, been Military and Civil Commandant, Military and Colonial Surgeon, Collector of Customs and held a few other offices, which he now divided with his colleague.

The civil appointments on the coast are wretchedly paid, but the military are in comparison better off, getting additional pay, and a great deal of long leave to England.

If the Gold Coast is to be governed eventually as a British possession, it must be done after the Indian manner, and our officers paid with Indian liberality.

In a short walk through the town with Doctor Goldsbury, we came across a grave dug in the middle of the street. A corpse was about to be buried in it, which the Doctor forbad, and the funeral party had to move elswhere and dig another grave. I was pointed out the ruined store-house, lately the property of Messrs. Swanzy, which had been destroyed when the fort had fired on the town. Doubtless the Dutch Commandant had his thoughts upon ridding himself of a powerful rival in trade when aiming at it. We went on to visit our loyal native friend, who gave us a welcome, took us into his upstairs front verandah and insisted on our drinking a bottle of excellent port wine which he produced; but port wine is not a refreshing beverage in Africa. The house although built in European style exteriorly, was kept and furnished in the interior after the native fashion of dirt and discomfort.

The country round Dix Cove is so densely covered with vegetation that it cannot be a healthy situation. The open sea before it is the only redeeming point. I was really sorry to leave Mr. Hughes there—he looked so delicate.

On the 4th August we arrived at Axim, which is to the westward of Cape Three Points. We towed Captain Hoare's brig, the *Alligator*, round with us. At Axim I was sorry to find that Captain Shepherd, the Commandant, had left for Cape Coast, very ill. Dr. Johnstone was Acting-Commandant, and the only white person in the place. He joined me as a fellow Commissioner, and our work began here.

Axim was an old Dutch settlement. The fort stands at the water's edge, the town running along in its rear. It was a slightly better residence than Dix Cove, but the accommodation was rough. Doctor Johnstone was of a happy disposition, and made the best of it, and found occupation in trying to perform the duties of the many offices which fell to his lot.

We summoned the King and Chiefs to meet us in the palaver hall of the fort the next morning at 10 a.m.

We did not get them there before noon, and Mr. Molenaar was surprised that we got them together then, as Africans don't understand being hurried.

They appeared with as long a "tail" of followers as any Highland Chiefs of old; the room was full. His Majesty was dressed in a handsome silk cloth, and a hat with red and white feathers, and the Dutch Royal arms in front, sandals on his feet, and an apron of leopard skin. He gave us a welcome and shook hands, as did two or three principal chiefs. Our party, consisting of Doctor Johnstone and myself, Commissioners; Mr. Yockney, H.M.S. *Torch*, Secretary; Mr. Molenaar, Interpreter and Assistant; and Captain Hoare, sat at a table at the head of the room; the Governor's stick-bearer and native interpreters behind us. Opposite, sat the King, his chiefs, stick bearer, public orator and "tail."

The stick bearer is the herald, and the stick he carries the known authority of his King. The sticks are canes, mounted in gold or silver.

Our message as spoken by me, was interpreted by our interpreter to the King's stick-bearer and orator, who delivered it again to the King, although he was within hearing all the time.

G

The reply was brought in the same round-about manner.

The King said that he wished for peace, and was willing to open the roads, but his western neighbour, Blay, Chief of the Ancobras, was a blackguard, who killed his men and stopped the road.

We said we would visit Blay; and asked him to send envoys with us to arrange terms of peace.

The King replied he would have no dealings with Blay who was a slave and no chief; the Ancobra country belonged to Amakee, King of Appolonia. Finally, however, it was agreed that the Axims would agree to any terms Amakee did.

It transpired that war had been going on for four years, ever since the transfer, and that Blay never paid tribute to the Dutch. Blay and his brother, Affoo, had been subjects of Amakee's. Affoo attained command of the army, rebelled and aspired to the throne. Amakee had to retreat to Assini in the French protectorate. Affoo burnt his town of Appolonia, then occupied by the Dutch, who garrisoned the fort, but on Affoo's approach abandoned the place. Affoo wrecked the fort, spiked the guns, and destroyed the carriages. He then retired to the stockaded town of Assama, further east. Amakee received assistance from Ashantee and advanced again, when some traitor in Affoo's camp cut off Affoo's head and sent it to Amakee, who thought the rebellion would be thus at an end, but Blay seized the stool, and had asserted his sovereignty over the district between the Ancobra river and Itanbo, and maintained it too, ever since, although both Ashantee and Axim had aided Amakee with troops.

We also learnt that during the previous May the British governors stick was sent to the Western chiefs to inform them of the transfer of the protectorate to us from the Dutch. Blay, to do honour to our Governor, sent two men to accompany the stick across the Ancobra. These men thinking the protection of the British herald pefectly sufficient were coming into Axim, when they were fallen upon, killed and decapitated within a mile of our fort. We told the King we should enquire into this matter, and arranged that we would go to Blay and Amakee and return to Axim after we had seen them.

Some of the Axims had not pleasing countenances. One chief wore a thick iron chain around his neck, and looked as if he could enjoy a tender steak from a deceased Ancobra! But these people have not been cannibals. I am told the King was in a fright all the time he was in the room, and was seen several times to shake in his Royal shoes.

CHAPTER V.

On the 6th August Mr. Molenaar and Captain Hoare
left Axim in hammocks for Blay's town of Assama.
The hammocks were carried by Captain Hoare's Kroomen, the Axims being afraid to cross the Ancobra.
The hammocks are slung from a bamboo, and are shaded
from the sun by an awning.   They were borne by four
men, other bearers following with the baggage; and
the same bearers will travel at the rate of four miles an
hour for twenty miles.   It is not an uncomfortable
mode of travelling.

Doctor Johnstone and I left in the *Torch* on the 7th
and arrived off Assama at 11 a.m. that day.   A large
red English ensign was flying over the town.   There
was a heavy sea, breaking far off shore, and a mist
rose from the breakers which is locally termed "the
smokes" rendering it difficult to discern anything distinctly on shore, although we were less than a mile
from it.   The rolling of the ship was very disagreeable.
Doctor Johnstone was anxious to land, so we determined to see what the surf boat could do.   We took
the precaution of putting on cork jackets, and I took

two good Kroomen in case of an accident. But we reached the shore safely, and found our colleagues comfortably housed in a clay built dwelling of several rooms, and furnished with a table or two, some chairs, and two bedsteads and mattrasses. They reported great enthusiasm along the road at the prospect of peace; no difficulties in travelling, except at the Ancobra, where the Axim boatmen were afraid to ferry them across, and boats had to be taken and pulled across by the Kroomen.

The house prepared for our reception was the best in Assama, and the furniture was all that could be collected in the town.

A palaver with Blay was arranged for the morrow. We were taken round the town and shown its defences, and told in what manner the Axims and Ashantees had been repulsed in their last attack. The stockade extends in a semi-circle from the sea by the rear of the town to the sea again. It consists of stout young palm trunks driven into the ground, and bound together with withies. At intervals of 100 yards are projections which are roofed over and thatched, and have two stories. The stockade is loopholed, and the men in these bastions are able to prevent an enemy getting near the stockade without great loss. Blays men said that the Axims lost more than a thousand men in one of their attempted assaults. The troops were drawn out for our inspection and went through some skirmishing drill, but before the palaver next day we had a grand review.

I had to return to the ship, but the rest of the party remained on shore that night. On landing again I was surprised to find a guard of five men in ragged red coats, caps of various colours and shapes, and trowsers of no colour or shape at all, who saluted me by presenting arms, giving the English words of command. I found they were troops belonging to the "Fantee Confederation," who had been sent to protect Blay! They were Cape Coast men, armed with percussion muskets, for which they had no caps. They appeared as if they had been near a rum cask that morning. One of them called himself "Colonel," and gave himself great airs, and us some trouble, and in the evening came for a "Dash" for his salute to us.

At 11 a.m. on the 8th we took our seats under some shady palms between the town and the stockade, a Krooman bearing the Union Jack before us; and our party was augmented by the Elmina boatmen and Captain Hoare's Kroomen who stood in our rear.

The troops, which yesterday were paraded and exercised on the sea beach, to-day defiled before us in companies of about 100 men strong, bearing "trade" guns,—flint-lock arms turned out at the rate of about five shillings each from Birmingham. They marched a few paces forward, when they had to halt to correct the formation, which was from three to six men deep.

The officer was assisted in this work by a "fetish" man or two, who ran along the ranks kicking or striking the shins of those out of place, or touching them up behind as the case might require. The commander of each company carried a skull in his mouth or by his side. The "fetish" man was whitewashed all over and wore a white cloth. Fetish women were also present, but did not take any active part in the performance. They wore white cloths, and were daubed over with white and red wash. Before each company was carried a small English flag, the staff of each being ornamented with the jawbones and fingers of fallen enemies. Each company acted independently. They were ordered to show us how they fought their last battle against the Axims.

Skirmishers were thrown out, by each company sending five front rank men at a run fifty paces to the front. These then threw themselves on the ground, and crawled cautiously forward. At a signal from one of their number, they raised their bodies, held their guns straight before them with both hands, shut their eyes and fired! They then scampered to the rear of their company as hard as they could go, and completed their loading. One squad of five, was quickly followed by another, until at length, with great shouting, beating of tom toms and sounding horns, a general firing took place, in no particular direction, all formation was lost, the poor fetish men became black again from perspiration, and the battle ended with the entire consumption of the stock of powder in Assama. Some few warriors, either better provided with ammunition, or slower in their movements than the others, continued the action on their own account for an hour after the main body had finished.

King Blay and his chiefs took their seats under trees 100 yards distant from us, and the male population of the town, and the warriors, formed a vast circle, the King's party and our party being at opposite ends of its diameter. Women and children crowded in the rear. The "Fantee guards" who had not condescended to take part in the review, helped to get people into their places, and the fetish men busied themselves doing the same thing near the king.

The ceremony opened by the King sending his orator and two stick bearers to bid us welcome, and say he would pay us a visit. We sent our stick bearer to say we should be glad to see him. He then crossed over to us followed by fifty chiefs or more. He wore a tall black hat, a very handsome silk cloth, and sandals.

He was a middle aged man, with an intelligent face and pleasant manner.

He shook hands, and all his staff followed, with whom we shook hands. Most of them said "How do!" or "Welcome!" (which grand word the "Fantee guards" taught them), or "Berry well." After this we paid the

King a visit, and more shaking hands took place. Then the King sent his "stick" as before, to ask if we had a message for him.

Mr. Molenaar, proceeded to give it, and took with him the presents. The quantity of each article given was pronounced aloud and repeated to the people, who cheered loudly at each announcement.

It was quite two hours before we could get to real business. We then requested the King to move near us so that we could speak face to face as friends. This, after consultation with the chiefs and Fetishmen, was agreed to, the people remained where they were, but the orator informed them from time to time, what matter was being discussed, and how business proceeded, The natives appeared to have good and accurate memories and some of our long addresses in English were, Molenaar said, translated readily without any part being forgotten.

Blay expressed himself quite ready to open the road and anxious for peace, but said that his neighbours were great rogues and it was their fault the roads were stopped. He complained of the Axims murdering his men who had accompanied Governor Ussher's stick, and impressed upon us that he had ever been loyal to the British flag, and had never fought under any other. He received a new flag from us with gladness and kissed it amid great cheers from his people.

He told us that he had been four years without

means of trading, as the Dutch had isolated his
territory, and that his people had only native made
cloth to clothe themselves with.

His cattle, sheep, and fields, had been destroyed by
his enemies. He now looked for our Governor's favour,
and vengeance on his enemies.

We promised to inform the Governor of what he
had told us; but informed him that even if his wishes
were not acceded to, he must not close the road by the
beach from Assini to Axim to travellers of any nation,
and as he and his nation had suffered so severely by
war, we recommended him to forget what was past,
and now that they were under one protectorate,
endeavour to live peaceably with their neighbours.

The people received this speech with applause.
They were evidently tired of war.

The King promised to send an embassy to Cape
Coast to settle small palavers, and after some little
trouble, promised hammock bearers to carry our party
to Appolonia if the *Torch* went there first, to warn
Amakee not to hurt them.

The "Colonel" of the "Fantee Guards" was very
anxious to turn our mission to his own account, by
asking us to insist that Blay should pay him better.

We recommended Blay to send him and his gallant
army home to Cape Coast; but Blay said the King of
Winnebah had sent them to him as a token of friend-
ship and he must keep them, although they must be

content with what pay he could afford. I believe this
consisted of a daily ration of Kanky and a few bananas.
To day the "Colonel" had been treated by the new
comers, or he had been looting during the sham fight,
for he was very drunk, and he was about the only
coast native I ever saw so.

These "Fantee guards" are a body of soldiers raised
by the confederated Fantee chiefs for defence of their
country against the Ashantees. The scheme for a
Fantee army, officered by educated natives, armed with
rifles and drilled like European soldiers, was a very
plausable one on paper. This is what it came to, in
fact. A few Cape Coast scapegraces got together, with
the knowledge of some words of command and how
to "stan at ease" and " present ups " like the sentries
at the Castle gate, and persuaded the native chiefs
they were trained soldiers. A subscription list was
sent round, and money . enough raised to buy a few
rifles. Their funds then failed. An appeal was made to
our government for assistance—our government declined.
The Governor was then requested to establish an
export duty on oil to support the Fantee army, but
this he refused to do. I have been informed, that in
the proposed scheme so much of the money to be
raised was allotted to the generals and staff-officers
that little was left for the rank and file ! We can now
tell very clearly what the Fantee army would have
been worth, from the wretched behaviour of the tribes,

educated and uneducated, in face of their Ashanti invaders.

Our palaver closed, with Blay again shaking hands.

He visited us afterwards at our quarters and presented us each with a gold ring of rough workmanship.

In the evening he paid us a private visit, and talked confidentially on political matters, told us we should find Amakee a great liar, and warned us not to believe a word he said. We said that Amakee would probably say the same thing of him, which produced a laugh.

He assured us that Amakee was in constant communication with Ashanti, that he had sent the whole of our Governor's late present to him and thirty female slaves to Ashanti, and that the king of Ashanti had sent 300 warriors to guard Amakee who were with him at the present time. He told us also that the king Axim was in treaty with Ashanti.

We slept very comfortably, with very little trouble from mosquitoes. The morning was quite chilly, and the natives wrapped their cloths closely round them and looked frozen.

We were up at daylight, and while we took a stroll round the town, our followers provided us a sumptuous breakfast, at which were one or two native luxuries, roasted plantains, kankee, and ground nut soup, the latter not at all bad.

The Commissioners embarked in the surf boat

immediately afterwards; the rest of the party starting in hammocks for Appolonia, 20 miles by land, and 12 miles by sea. There were more volunteers as carriers than could be employed, and the impression produced on our minds by the conduct of the people was that an immense load of care had been removed from their shoulders.

Trade began briskly with goods from the *Alligator*, and I saw our Elmina boatmen were prepared for a trading expedition, and had small quantities of goods to sell for gold. Every native appeared to have a pinch of gold dust wrapped up in some part of his cloth, and they were anxious to exchange it for tobacco, cloth, or powder.

Before leaving, Blay asked us to give him back the powder his troops fired at the review as he had none left. We consented.

We were much amused at the caution taken by the gold buyers against fraud. Captain Hoare informed me that it was very dangerous for a white man to buy gold on his own judgment.

He, and nearly all traders on the coast employed native assayers, who are held responsible that nothing but the pure metal is purchased. These men put the gold offered for sale into a copper pan, they shake it about and blow it to remove all dust and dirt, then with a feather they remove such particles as do not please the eye, and return them to the seller, as it is

possible they are of pure gold, but much oftener they
are brass filings; then the assayer rubs the rest of the
dust on a stone, and unless it produces a certain colour
on that, the whole lot is rejected.   In this manner
traders are seldom imposed upon with rubbish, but
without proper precautions they are certain to be.

The gold for sale all consists of dust.   Nuggets are
obliged to be sent to the chiefs.   It comes in very
small quantities, often only an "akie" or two at a time.
An "akie" is an accacia seed weighing a few grains.
Accounts with natives on this coast are all kept in
"ounces."   That is, ounces of gold.   The value given
is about £3 an ounce in goods, but of course this is
only nominal.   Captain Hoare called it a "clean trade,"
but said there was not such a large profit as is sometimes derived from oil.

If permanent peace was established the whole
country between the Ancobra and Assinie is likely to
become wonderfully productive.

CHAPTER VI.

THE *Torch* anchored off Appolonia at noon. Owing to "the smokes" it was difficult to distinguish the town. Had it not been for the fort which is much higher than the native houses, we might have passed it.

The swell was very heavy.

We took the usual precautions, when landing, but the rollers were breaking at quite one-third of a mile off shore, and if the " padron" of the surf boat had not felt confident of his skill, we should not have attempted it.

We passed the first breaker successfully, but the second one came into the boat, filled her, and she sank under our feet. Fortunately she kept upright, and the water was so shallow that we could feel her with our toes. The first few seas set us fast towards the shore, boat and all, then a current carried us along to the eastward. The heavy seas striking down on our heads had a stunning effect, and I saw the Doctor's head droop from exhaustion. Fearing he would drown, I directed Tom Peters and Jack Smart, the Kroomen from the *Torch* I had brought with me, to assist him; but nothing could induce these men to leave the

"Cap'en." One had my sword, and the other a bag of
signal flags under the off arm ; with the other they
supported me. I could swim, and told them so, but
they would not leave me. By jumping to the seas,
springing up from the thwarts of the sunken boat, as
the seas reached us, we saved ourselves a little. Johnstone rallied and was able to do this. The crew of the
boat were swimming near the boat, but not helping us.
We saw the *Torch's* boat approach the edge of the
surf but she dare not enter. Looking landwards we
were cheered to see numerous black heads rapidly near-
ing us, and a number of small canoes on their way to
our rescue. The latter reached us first and I was delighted to see Johnstone tumbled into one, although
he was more dead than alive. I was soon taken by
another and paddled quickly on shore. The swimmers
who had so readily taken to the water to assist us were
quite fifty in number, and neither they nor the canoemen asked for any reward.

It was calculated we were twenty minutes in the
water. My colleague's peril was imminent, but once on
shore he speedily recovered. Our loss in property was
serious. We had provisions for our large party for four
days in the boat, our clothes and other necessaries ; some
of them were saved, and the surf boat was eventually
got on the beach and rolled to a place of safety. The
" Padron " complained that all the gold realized by the
crew at Assama went to the bottom. I doubted him,
but said " serve you right."

We found ourselves received with open arms by a white person, Mr. Novi, a Spanish gentleman, agent for the French house of Vardier & Co., who took us to his house, furnished us with a fresh water bath, men to rub us with coarse towels until we were in a glow, and then lent us flannel clothing and gave us a glass of cordial. The king sent to express his gratification at our safety and to offer assistance. Finding that his canoemen were not afraid to go through the surf to the *Torch,* we sent Jack Smart to the ship for clothes and provisions. In due time these arrived, carefully tied up in waterproof bags. Mr. Novi, and those competent to judge, said that our boat filled entirely from want of skill. Yet the boats used here were different from ours, they were shorter and much lighter, with only four paddlers.

The party travelling by land did not arrive until 7 p.m. King Amakee immediately he was informed by us they were coming, sent a large armed escort to Itanbo to bring them in, and carry the hammocks if the Assama men were afraid to come in, but at sunset his men returned, our party not being in sight. Very shortly after they came up, and without any hesitation, the Assama men came straight into town. To our astonishment they appeared to receive a hearty welcome. The Appolonians were evidently anxious for peace also.

A grand dance was performed outside our quarters

H

by torchlight—the music consisted mostly of "tom-tom," the native drum. The dancers formed a circle and kept good time in their movements of hands and feet, and chanted some refrain all the time. The performers were all men or boys, and they kept it up until late in the night.

Mr. Yockney and the shore party reported highly of their reception at the villages they passed through. At every mile or two fresh carriers fought for the honour of carrying them, and at several places refreshments were provided.

Mr. Novi was not able to put all our party up, although he made his house stretch to an astonishing extent. It was only a native one made of palm stems and thatched with leaves, but it was quite weather proof and airy. We slept in hammocks.

Mr. Novi was the only white man in the place. He told us he lived in the native fashion, on kanky, plantains, and water, with occasionally a little fish as a relish, and that he found that diet agree with him very well.

Captain Hoare had a room of his own fitted up and always kept ready in the house of Taniki, the King's nephew, who acted as Captain Hoare's local agent.

Mr. Molenaar found accommodation at a Chief's house.

The early morning was chilly as at Assama. This was owing I think to "the smokes;" the suspended

moisture in the atmosphere, which causes this phenomenon, penetrating the low-laying houses. Our house
being close to the sea, there appeared no chance of our
clothes getting dry.

Before breakfast we went for a walk. The town
was not large, the houses were new, and the streets
wider and straighter than usual. The fort was grass
grown, and falling to ruin, but a moderate sum would
put it in repair. The rooms were large and airy, the
situation good, and we had a pleasant walk on its roof,
above the " smokes."

As usual in native towns the sanitary customs were
abominable. The well in the fort from which the
drinking water was taken, was half filled with rubbish
and filth. The smells on the beach and in rear of the
town were dreadful, and our appetite was not improved
by our walk. Tom Peters, who acted as our cook still
further tried it by cooking a dish of his own composing.
Sardines and Oxford sausages boiled together in an
earthern pot ! The shock to our nerves at first sight of
this uninviting dish was great, but the sausages proved
eatable.

Amakee sent to say that it was impossible he could
get his chiefs together before the next day, the 11th, at
10 a.m. for which hour the palaver was fixed.

During the day we received private visits from
several chiefs, among others from the Ashantee
Commander of the party mentioned by Blay. He was

H 2

a fine manly fellow and we at once took a great fancy
to him.

He had the manners of a gentleman and all the
bearing of a soldier, was well dressed, and without
followers. He said his men were in the bush, and he
had not brought them, and did not intend to bring
them into the town, that his object was to trade, but
Ashantees always carried their guns.

Taniki the King's nephew, talks English very well.
He talked temperately of local politics, expressed himself anxious for peace, and to see a British Commandant
in the fort once more, and said it was a bad thing for
the Appolonians we ever had left.

During the day the warriors were exercised on the
beach as at Assama, and armed escorts were sent out to
meet the chiefs coming from a distance, and bring them
in with honour. The troops were kept in the same
formation as at Assama, and the skirmishing was
performed in the same manner. The companies carried
Dutch colours; the staves were more profusely ornamented with fingers and jawbones than at the other
place, and a strong net full of skulls was carried on a
pole by two men before each company. Some of the
warriors were boys of 12 or 14 years of age.

Most of the men who appeared to be officers carried
skulls smeared with blood, and they ornamented themselves with jaw bones and fingers. The soldiers carried
their powder in two calabashes slung from their

shoulders, one containing coarse powder to load with, and the other finer for priming. The troops remained on the beach all day, and firing never ceased until sunset.

We walked out to Itanbo in the evening. The people eastward of this point refuse to acknowledge Amakee's authority and are Blay's loyal subjects. It was once a large town, but Affoo burnt it at the same time he destroyed Appolonia. As Amakee was taken by surprise then, he keeps an armed guard continually, whose duty it is to signal the approach of an enemy, and keep them in check until the warriors are assembled. Itanbo is only two miles from Appolonia.

The next morning at daylight everyone was astir. The warriors assembled near the King's house. The women were set to work to cut down the grass in front of the fort, where the "palaver" was to be held. The streets were swept up, rubbish removed, and everything put in order. We noticed that at every entrance into the town, balls of kanky and jars of palm wine or water, were placed to refresh friends from a distance. Appolonia is not stockaded, so I mean by "entrances" where the paths entered the town. Men and women turned out in their smartest attire. A Chief living next door to us wore a French grey ribbed silk, that must have cost much money. Taniki paid us an early visit, wearing still more expensive and brighter silk. A Wassaw chief sat opposite our door in a chair of

state, covered in gold, and wearing scarlet and gold
clothes and handsome ornaments. His followers
formed a circle before him. In the middle, two men
performed antics intended for dancing. A huge " tom
tom," six feet long and about eighteen inches in
diameter, was borne on the head of one slave and
beaten with two sticks by another. It was formed out
of the hollowed trunk of a tree and covered with skin,
ornamented with snakes, skins and human bones.
Occasionally a horn struck up, to disturb the monotonous sound of the " tom tom," which for about two
hours never ceased to sound. All this time the old
Chief sat still, never moving a muscle, but looking very
important.

At ten a.m. the palaver took place. It was on a
much larger scale than at Assama, and much more
brilliant. Chairs were provided for our party close to
the walls of the fort. To our astonishment, we found
the " Colonel" from Assama placed behind us; but in
mufti! We found afterwards that several Cape Coast
men, and men from eastern tribes had mixed themselves with our native followers, to spy and report our
proceedings to their Chiefs.

Amakee was more royally arrayed than any native
King I had yet seen, and had a large red umbrella held
over his head. Several other chiefs also had umbrellas,
and in one instance a woman held it. Tanaki sat on
the King's right, and the chief men of the State close

around him. The preliminary proceedings were of the same kind as at Assama. Such a day of handshaking I have never been through before, or since. After the King's visit had been paid, and returned, the Ashantee and Wassaw Chiefs performed the same ceremony, and it had to be returned. The executioner, a hideous creature naturally, but with his face and body painted to add to his disgusting appearance, carried a large sheathed knife before the Ashantee Chief. The Wassaw Chief was carried on the heads of slaves in a coffin-shaped box, covered with a very rich cloth. There was another Chief present, who brought a young, well-dressed woman, evidently a person of importance, but not his wife, with him. She did not shake hands, and looked frightened. We saw several women standing near the central group that surrounded the king.

To forward business, we dispensed with the ordinary method of speaking through the public orators, and spoke face to face, first in English, which Taniki translated to the people, and then it was repeated in the native language by Mr. Molenaar.

The people all listened attentively, and occasionally said words of approval or otherwise. We gave the king an English flag, and read out a list of the presents which were on board the *Alligator* for him, as unfortunately the brig had not arrived.

The King's answer to us was to this point. He was

glad to receive the English flag again, and would be loyal to it. He had never wished to change it for the Dutch, but he had not been consulted. He did what the English told him. The road along the beach should be open where his authority was respected; he could not answer for it elsewhere. He should be glad of peace, for war had made him poor, but Blay was a slave, and the son of a slave, and he would not treat with him. He denied sending our Governor's present, or the slaves to Ashantee. The present had only given a silver ring to each of his head men, and he complained that our Governor sent as much to Blay as to him.

In the end we were enabled to obtain from the King a promise not to attack Blay, to send an embassy to Cape Coast, and to open the road at once. This was as much as we could expect. The King expressed a hope that Appolonia would be made a port of entry, and have a resident English Commandant.

The result of the palaver seemed satisfactory to all parties, and Amakee said he should send his son with the embassy to Cape Coast to represent him.

Before we left Appolonia an embarrassing circumstance occurred. In Mr. Novi's house was stored a quantity of trade goods, which had not paid duty. A notice had been posted at Cape Coast ever since the western districts came under our protection, that vessels trading, or traders importing goods anywhere, but at a port of entry, should be liable to a fine of £500.

As Captain Hoare was obliged to pay duty on his goods, he naturally drew attention to the fact that his rival in trade had not done so, and Dr. Johnstone, in his capacity as Collector of Customs, was obliged to call upon our kind host to obey the law. This was done, but shortly afterwards the King sent to request us to remit it as he would practically have to pay the duty, and he had received no pecuniary advantage as yet from our protection. There was logic in his argument, and we took it upon ourselves to remit the tax. Amakee also very sensibly remarked that if we collected a tax on goods imported into his dominions, it is only fair that he should benefit by it in the way of protection, and the money ought not to be spent on improvements at Cape Coast and Elmina.

As the current on the Coast of Guinea runs strongly to the East, and the wind blows almost constantly towards the same point, it is very difficult for sailing vessels to get to the West again, once they have passed eastwards. Consequently Appolonia lost considerably by not being a port of entry, for it was 20 miles to windward of Axim, where a vessel had to go to enter before she could discharge a bale of cloth at Appolonia. All this we mentioned to the Governor in our report.

Before leaving, Amakee presented us with gold rings, two splendid sheep, and some vegetables. The sheep produced as good mutton as it was possible to eat.

Mr. Novi showed us a quantity of "pawn gold" in his possession. This consists of ornaments, deposited with the traders as security for goods given on credit. Some of these were heavy gold chains, gold plates worn as marks of distinction by the Chiefs, and "fetish" charms shaped like men and animals. Some of the work on these ornaments was well done, other was very coarse.

Mr. Novi had been to Coomassie, he walked all the way. I heard some stories of the King of Ashanti, in his house if not from him.

It is said to be etiquette at the Ashanti court to watch attentively the King's face, to laugh when he laughs, be grave when he is so ; and I was told that even a prisoner about to be sent to death would follow this rule if the King smiled as he announced the sentence.

If a man tells a story which makes the King laugh, the king will take a handful of gold from a jar by his side, and send it to the joker.

I heard it said that the Ashantees made a great profit in trading with the tribes to the north of them, sometimes exchanging powder with them for its weight in gold.

We embarked in safety, using the boat we were capsized in, but a crew of Captain Hoare's men. The *Torch* then returned to Axim.

At Axim we had a final palaver, at which Amakee's terms were agreed to. The road was to be open to all from Assini to Axim. The tribes were not to attack one another without first appealing to Cape Coast, and representatives were to be sent to Cape Coast to settle some petty complaints. We gave the King a good lecture on his behaviour in murdering Blay's men. When we called on him to explain his conduct, he said he was at war with Blay, and considered it fair to kill his men whenever he could !

When the palaver was about to break up, the King handed us a 6-lb. shot and said it was one of two that was fired into his house at 9 o'clock the previous night, from a gun of the fort. A nine o'clock gun is fired every night, but of course it ought to be a blank one.

Immediate enquiry was made, and we found that a soldier of the 2nd West had been seen to put something into the gun, and others had seen two shot in his possession.

It was now our turn to apologise to the King. We took the mischief-making soldier to Cape Coast as a prisoner.

A native committed suicide in the town. Doctor Johnstone was "Coroner" as well as everything else, and had to preside at an inquest and give medical evidence as well to the jury There was no reason to be . found for the deed, except that the wives of the deceased had been quarrelling. He shot himself in the head, firing the gun with his toe which he had tied to the trigger of a gun. The body, having been white-washed by the fetish man, was laid out in the centre of the village for all the people to see, and in the course of a few hours was buried. On the 14th August we returned to Cape Coast Castle.

In reporting our proceedings to the Governor we were able to say that the object of our mission had been accomplished; but that both Mr. Molenaar and Captain Hoare were of opinion that the natives could not be depended on to perform their promise to keep peace with their neighbours unless they took the native oath between them.

We also drew attention to one or two matters which were well known at Cape Coast, which kept the native mind in a state of uneasiness. One of these was that an Ashantee Chief, named Atchampong, had brought a force of 2,000 men to aid the Elminas in 1870. This man remained at Elmina up to the time of the transfer, but as the Dutch did not think it right he should fall into our hands he was taken to Assini. His men would not follow him, but settled near Elmina. The Chief said his honour forbade him to return to Ashantee without his men, so he continued to plot with, and disturb, the Western tribes, and he has had much to do with what has since occurred. We also remarked upon the extreme jealousy existing between tribes formerly under different protections, and the necessity of endeavouring to reconcile them.

CHAPTER VII.

I HAD knocked my leg against the boat, at the capsize off Appolonia, and the wound ulcerated. The climate is a very bad one for ulcers. We found much more trouble from this than from fever. Captain Nelson was good enough to take me on board the *Druid* for a change. In a fortnight I was well again.

The *Druid's* officers amused themselves by butterfly hunting, and had made some good collections.

The *Bittern* and *Coquette* arrived, and there were some cricket matches, and no one was the worse for playing in the hot sun.

The first day I was able to land we found the town in a state of commotion. Drums were beating and processions marching. We were told the companies were electing new Captains. The towns on the Gold Coast are divided into companies. At Cape Coast there are twelve; at Elmina, ten; at Accra, ten; at Axim, two; and so on. The companies generally have distinct occupations, as fishermen, surf-boatmen, labourers and their families, etc. Calling at Dr. Rowe's house he told us he had just been visited by an

unprotected female, a native lady, who called on him
to protect her from a mob which filled his courtyard.
Without asking questions, the Doctor took down his
whip, and in a few seconds the rabble had disappeared.
The lady then explained to him that it was her company who wished to make her Captain ; an honour she
declined to accept, and they had endeavoured to force
it upon her; and to carry her through the town on
men's shoulders.   The lady was the daughter of the
late Captain who had died a few months ago without
sons.   In such cases the daughters often succeed them,
especially if they have money, but this lady said as she
had two elder sisters in the town the company had no
business to elect her.   The greatest objection she offered
to the proposed honour was, that it would be so expensive : as she would be expected to sit in state and provide gin for all who were presented to her.   Besides,
she said she was going to marry a man in No. 3 company, and wished to say good-bye to No. 2 altogether !
We heard a story explaining why fishermen will not
fish on Tuesday.   I had thought that it was for some
religious reason, but Mrs. Barnes told us that there is a
tradition at Cape Coast that a fisherman once caught
a mermaid on a Tuesday, and since then the day has
been " fetish" to them, and they dare not put hook or
net in the water on that day lest a similar evil befall
them.

   The master of a Danish brig was drowned at

Annamaboe, landing in a surf boat, and close to the shore. It is supposed sharks took him, for the surf was not bad, and the kroomen lost sight of him very quickly. Although men are often in the water on this coast, I did not hear of any other accidents from sharks. I think large sharks like less troubled waters, and that the best feeding grounds for them are near the mouths of rivers. Lagos has such a bad repute for the number and voracity of sharks on the bar, that some kroomen will not engage as boatmen to factors there at all; and they always make the fact of the danger to their lives from sharks if capsized, a plea for claiming higher wages. The largest sharks we saw were off St. Paul's de Loanda.

We left Cape Coast on the 9th September for what is called the "South Coast," that is the southern division of the West African Station. Its limits are between Cape Lopez and the 20th parallel of south latitude.

It has always been considered the best part of the station, as being healthier, having better harbours, a better climate and better markets than in the "Bights." The "Bights" division extends from Cape Lopez to Cape Palmas, and derives its name from the Bights of Benin and Biafra, which are included within its limits.

We enjoyed most lovely sailing between Jellah Coffee and Kabenda. Our course took us close to the island of St. Thomas, a Portuguese possession of some importance. It produces excellent coffee and cocoa. We passed at about three miles from the town, which appeared of considerable size, with one or two large forts to protect it. The island rises to about 8000 feet in height, and on its south-western side shows some curious formations. One natural pillar rises from the hill side like a great factory chimney. At Prince's Island, a few miles north of St. Thomas are similar protuberances which look like bullock horns.

We found Kabenda looking very different to what it was in April. The trees were without leaves, and the long grass burnt up into very dry hay by the long drought. The fields were clear of crops, but the fruit was ripe and we got excellent mangoes, guavas, bananas and limes. The paths were much more pleasant to walk upon, and at Kabenda there are paths in many directions. However, the rains had just set in, so we went away to the south as soon as the business I had to do would allow. I made a short call at the Congo, and on the 26th September anchored off Ambrizette. At Sharks point King Peter was very pressing for a "dash," as the Burial ground was in such good order. I pointed out to him I had nothing with me in the boat to "dash" him, and that he must wait until I came again, when he replied "Give me shilling for buy chop." "Chop" is African for something to eat.

At Ambrizette were five British, one Dutch, and one French factory. Our countrymen were very glad to see us, and most pressing for us to remain. They took us over their stores, and showed us some large tusks of ivory. They valued it at about 4s. 6d. a lb. on the spot and at 8s. in England. The largest in store weighed 8-lbs., and was 6 feet in length. The merchants had purchased tusks weighing 150-lbs., and had heard of a pair weighing 187-lbs. and 189-lbs, respectively. The tusks were black outside, but the black scale is very thin. Legitimate trade had only existed at Ambrizette for five years. Previously it had only exported slaves. The exporters were Portuguese, but the importers of goods were British, Dutch, and French. They sold goods to the Portuguese, and the Portuguese purchased slaves with the goods. The slaves used to carry a little ivory with them from the interior, but it was a very small quantity compared with what comes down now.

The European goods I saw in the stores consisted of cotton cloths of a flimsy quality, and handkerchiefs; guns and pistols, with flint locks of course; gunpowder; brass and copper rods; brass rings for women's ankle ornaments; glass beads, knives, padlocks, and a lot of trash.

I was told that some old French and German uniforms had been well disposed of. The traders kept some small articles "for top" which always closes a bargain.

These were snuff boxes, looking glasses, and toys.

I

"Jack in the box" was said to be most popular. But I have omitted to state that the trade article most in demand was spirits. Rum and gin were equally popular, equally bad, and equally profitable. In return, the merchants obtained besides ivory, pea nuts, gum copal, wax, and a little India rubber. I obtained some good specimens of malachite recently brought in from a village close to.

The following afternoon we reached St. Paul's de Loanda, the capital of the Portuguese province of Angola, and the residence of the Governor-General. The port is formed by a sand bank which runs parallel to the coast for many miles, having deep water at its eastern entrance between the bank and the main land, which are from one to two miles distant from each other. When St. Paul's is reached the harbour gets suddenly shallow and vessels have to anchor two miles below the town, but in perfect security. The bank mentioned rises a few feet above water, and palms and bushes grow on it. The Government dockyard is built on that side and several neat villas belonging to the aristocracy of St. Paul's. The main land consisted of steep red cliffs, looking very bare of vegetation at this time. The city is built partly at the foot and partly on the top of this cliff. The buildings are of stone or brick, the streets are wide and macadamized, with paved side paths in some places. There are several churches, barracks, and large public buildings. The

Governor-General's palace is on the high ground, and occupies a large amount of space. It is most comfortably furnished, and His Excellency frequently opened his ball room doors for entertainments. An excellent band played in front of the palace every evening. The attendance at its performance was never large during our stay.

I saw several neat carriages drawn by horses or mules; but the ordinary cab of St. Paul's is the Maxina—pronounced Mashena—which is a kind of palanquin, carried by two negroes. The seat is very low. It consists of a frame with cane work, about six feet long, on which you rest your legs, and an arm and back to lean against, with an awning overhead and curtains to draw at option on either side. White men or half-castes never seemed to go ten paces except in one of these things.

The shops were very good, but their articles exorbitantly dear. Market produce was dear on account of a civil war then proceeding in the interior. The position of affairs at St. Paul's had been very critical a few months previously. The city is entirely supplied with drinking water from a river seven miles distant. The natives for a short time got possession of it. If they could have held it the consequences would have been fearful.

As it was there was great distress among the poor of Loanda. Marrioc and beans, their staple food, were

I 2

at four times their usual price. Bread was 8½d. a lb.
and beef 7d., which is double what it used to be. In
the shops we paid 3s. 6d. a lb. for butter and 2s. 6d. a
lb. for bacon.

The province produces excellent coffee, and there is
a large trade in it to Europe. The river Coanza enters
the sea about 100 miles from St. Paul's, to the south-
ward. In the dry season the bar of this river becomes
impassable, at times drying right across. In the rainy
season there is water enough for small steamers to cross,
and they ascend the river for more than 100 miles. I
am told that this Coanza country is one of the most
lovely and fertile in Africa. The Portuguese, however,
have not turned it to account as they might have,
the natives hate them, and they hate the natives.
Loanda is a penal colony. The convicts are given a
ticket-of-leave, after they have served a certain time in
the local army, and few of them return to Portugal.
I saw some of these troops marching in from the
Coanza. They were decently clothed in a brown uniform, but badly armed with different pattern muskets;
and I noticed one man had no lock to his. Angola has
to support itself; and its treasury is not always full,
so I suppose there has been a difficulty in providing
arms for the soldiers, the mother country so plentifully
supplies! The Governor told us he had ordered 1500
Martini-Henry rifles, to enable the troops to put down
the present war.

Mr. Hartley, our vice-consul, had been 14 years in Africa. He had been for a considerable time in the distant interior, elephant hunting. He was sometimes two years without seeing a white man, or speaking a word of English. He spoke highly of the treatment he received from the natives. The Hottentots were the only people he had trouble with, and he narrowly escaped with his life from their hands.

There were three English ladies in St. Paul's! Of course there are many Portuguese, and still more of Creole ladies.

The city is called healthy, but it is liable to epidemics. Fevers and small-pox create ravages among natives and Europeans. I observed some drainage works in progress and imagine they were wanted.

An English steamer calls here once a month. She calls all along the coast on her outward voyage, turns round at St. Paul's and returns the same way. A Portuguese steamer sails once a month for Lisbon, *viâ* St. Thomas, Princes, and St. Vincent (Cape Verdes).

A differential system of duties excludes all foreign ships from any share in the carrying trade from this province. The venality of officials, especially those connected with the Customs is openly spoken of. The hindrance to trade by the formalities and absurd regulations, all to be avoided by paying a small bribe to someone, is greatly complained of. Labour was getting much more expensive. Slavery in every shape was being gradually abolished, and I heard many doubts expressed whether the Portuguese would retain Angola for many years.

We arrived at Elephant Bay, a place in the Portuguese territory in latitude 14° south, longitude 12° east, on the 8th of October, for the purpose of refitting the ship. It is on the northern edge of the rainless region of South Africa. Rain does not fall there for sometimes three or four years, and consequently there is very little verdure, but the wide and deep water courses, the serated appearance of the hills, and the mass of *debris* in the valleys, show that when the rain does come there is plenty of it.

Elephant bay is perfectly sheltered from the prevailing wind which is from the south. It is situated at the north side of an extensive valley, which is surrounded by hills varying in height from 800 to 1500 feet. In the water courses are clumps of thorny bushes on which the antelopes and zebras feed, and there is a spring of brackish water near the beach to which they resort for drink.

No inhabitants reside nearer than at Equamina, which was four miles from our anchorage by sea, and twice that distance by land. At Equamina is a large farm for growing sugar cane from the juice of which a large quantity of aquadiente is distilled.

The valley runs back for some miles, affording good hard level walking ground. Everywhere it was marked with tracks of the zebras, which come to drink at the springs, but we never saw any of them, although some of the officers lay out at night near the springs, and set traps for them.

Antelopes, gazelles, and jackals were seen, but were all very shy and difficult to approach. We were told that lions came down occasionally, after rain, but as a rule they were not met within fifty miles of the place.

We landed the men under tents, and cleared the ship out, to get clear of the cockroaches which had begun to get large in size and very numerous. The men enjoyed the fun extremely. In the evening they played cricket or rounders; or else went fishing with the seine. The quantity of fish in the bay is marvellous. One draw of the net was generally sufficient for the whole crew, and occasionally there were many more than required. The fish consisted chiefly of mullet and bream, but now and then there were some very large species.

Sperm whales were constantly in the bay, and would come close round the ship at times. American vessels come to this coast to fish for them.

On the hill side to the west of us were the names of the men-of-war that had visited the bay, marked in whitewash. Some of the letters are more than 50 feet long, and they can be seen at a great distance. As some of them had been done for years, not much rain could have fallen during that period. We remained here until the 28th October and enjoyed our visit very much. We found Senhor Pina and his wife always delighted to see us when we went to Equamina. They literally turned their house inside out to entertain us. Equamina valley is separated from Elephant bay by a steep spur of mountain land that juts into the sea, over which it was a stiff climb. By taking advantage of the alternate land and sea breezes the passage is a pleasant one in a boat, but the beach is not protected from the ocean swell as at Elephant bay, and the landing is not good. Senhor Pina's plantation and house are close to the beach. The latter is a one-storied building of four or five rooms, in connection with the farm buildings. It was plain enough, but comfortable, and the Senhora had managed to transport a grand piano to this out-landish spot. The farm consisted of about 200 acres under sugar cane, and a large garden containing vegetables and fruit trees. There was also enough grass about to feed a small herd of cattle, and flocks of sheep and goats managed to thrive on the wild bush.

The farm is artificially irrigated. Water is found all over this valley at a few feet from the surface, but this is, as a rule, slightly brackish, although there are wells of excellent drinking water. The labourers were slaves: 200 were employed, men and women. They seem very happy, living in native houses by themselves, each family having a piece of ground to grow vegetables on, and they had two free days a week

—Saturday and Sunday—when they could fish or do what they liked. Besides, they had a regular daily ration of beans, fish, and aquadiente. This latter stimulant they will drink as much of as they can get, the women as well as the men. On Sunday they have a double ration. It is a very strong spirit, but not strong enough for them, and we were told they were in the habit of mixing chillies with the raw aquadiente to make it "bite" harder. They appeared to be kept strictly to task, and I am afraid Lynch law was the common one of the land.

On account of the vegetation, this valley is much more frequented by game than Elephant bay. Our first report of it was that it teemed with game. One of our officers shot a large Koodoo, which produced 600 lbs. of meat. Excellent meat it was too. We saw a fair number of these animals, but found them most difficult to stalk even with the assistance of native trackers. The ground was covered with clumps of trees, between which were wide spaces to walk on, on which the fresh footprints could easily be seen. The Koodoos ran at great speed and made for the hills immediately they were alarmed. At a distance they looked like red deer.

Early one morning we met a large number of Baboons, who howled hideously as they fled up the rocks, the old ones carrying the young on their backs.

Senhor Pina supplied us with good beef, mutton,

and vegetables during our stay, and now and then a
little fruit.   He grows a few grapes but they were not
in season.

At times he has apples and pears, peaches and
olives, besides mangoes, oranges, limes, and bananas.

The cabbages attain a very large size, and potatoes
are sometimes grown.

There is a distillery on the premises, for producing
the aquadiente.   None of the cane juice is made into
sugar, as spirit making pays best.

The Senhor also salted a large quantity of fish for
the St. Paul's market, and he manufactured bricks and
tiles, and burnt lime for the same purpose.

The dinner at which we were entertained, introduced
us to some novel dishes.   It consisted of cabbage soup,
boiled veal, bacon and vegetables cut up together; a
chicken pie; a savoury stew of kid, with plenty of
garlic ; a kind of beef olive—more garlic ; patties of
salt meat, with sugar; cuttle fish stewed in wine; a
stuffed fish, baked ; roast veal and fried potatoes ; boiled
potatoes ; cheese made of goats' milk ; olives ; jellies ;
open tarts, and a kind of custard pudding which nearly
did for me, after tasting some of the strange and
unaccustomed dishes my curiosity led me to ascertain
the nature of.   The only part of the banquet I can pro-
nounce an entire failure was, the boiled potatoes, and
the Senhora told us that neither she nor her servants
could succeed in boiling them so that they should be

eatable. I never knew that there was so much of an art in boiling potatoes before. But there is : our cook sent the same kind of potatoes to table like balls òf flour. We were waited upon by five women servants. each with a baby clinging to its mother's back.

Senhora Pina had a half-caste lady residing with her, as a companion, and a pet slave child was allowed to play about the sitting room. There were two or three white men on the plantation besides Senhor Pina.

Before we left, our friends paid us a visit on board the *Torch,* and they were I dare say, as much astonished at an English dinner, as we had been at a Portugese one. Mustard and plum pudding they did not at all like, but they were in raptures with our potatoes.

On the 30th October we arrived at Benguela which is 100 miles North of Elephant Bay. It is a convict station. The houses are all low, the streets wide and clean, but there is little business doing. There were a great many natives from the interior in the town; a low type of mankind—dirty and ugly. One man wore his hair plaited into a pig tail with a bell at the end of it.

They had bows, arrows, spears, and native axes, Knobberies and ornaments to sell, and would take English money. Small boys brought us beautiful little birds in wicker cages, and warranted songsters called "Benguelenas," which have a note like a canary's. We saw a few good leopard skins but they were very dear.

There is a good market and a few fair shops in the town. The country around looked barren, but rain was expected, and after it came the ground would be very productive. Good cattle are reared.

The white convicts work on the public works without chains, and after a very short residence, become soldiers, convict guards, or are allowed to settle as tradesmen or shopkeepers, or hire themselves to planters as overseers. They are an ill-looking set. The black convicts were chained together in gangs of half-a-dozen. They had an iron ring round their necks, and a chain shackled to it by which they were fastened to each other. The overseer, a "degredado," or ex-convict, over each batch of six, was armed with a strong cane. The men carried baskets of stone, mortar or rubbish on their heads. Some of them wore leg irons as an additional punishment. A few of the negro convicts are conditionally at large. They must be inside the fort between 8 p.m. and 6 a.m.

As I was returning from the Governor's house to my boat, 1 was accosted by one of these convicts at large. He made a statement to me which I will repeat in full, as it tells its own story. It was made on oath, before me, on the 30th October, 1872.

" I, Joseph Hardy, was born at Sierra Leone in 1843. My parents were Liberians, and live now at Cape Palmas. I lived at Sierra Leone for two years after I was born, and subsequently for six years working for Mr. George Hedley. I shipped as a sailor on board the *Albatross*, of Liverpool, in 1865, and went to Gaboon, where I was discharged, and served with a trading master (factor) for three years, and afterwards at Brooklyn, Camma, for two years; I then returned to Gaboon and shipped in an Italian barque bound for Loanda. I was discharged there with three others, without wages, because we claimed to be sent to Gaboon, as the Captain had promised, but he wished us to go to Brazil. I complained to a Custom House officer, but he said he could do nothing for me. As one of our number was an American we went to the American consul, but he said, as we had no written agreement with the Captain he could not help us.

I could not obtain employment at Loanda, and I sold my kit to support myself. I slept on the beach. I had only 3s. 6d. left, when, as I was walking along the streets a policeman came and searched me all over, took my money, and told me to go away. I asked him to give me the money back, when he took me to prison. I was perfectly sober at the time. After three days I asked to see the magistrate. I was taken before him, and by him sent to the Governor's office, where some papers were written and I was sent to the fort. A chain was put round my neck and I was fastened to other prisoners. I remained there three months at hard labour.

As I did not understand Portuguese, I did not

know what was said; but after this I learnt enough to make my wants known. I asked permission to work outside. I told them I could do cooper's work, but the Governor ordered me to be sent to Benguella where I arrived on the 10th December, 1870. The chain was taken off my neck, previous to leaving Loanda. At Benguella I was paid 6d. a day for my work, but was obliged to find my own food and clothing, and to sleep in the fort. I was obliged to be in the fort at 8 p.m., and was locked up until 6 a.m. the next day. I worked from 6 a.m. until 6 p.m. except for 2 hours in the middle of the day. I did not wear any chains, but was kept a prisoner. I was flogged 5 or 6 times over the back with a thick stick, receiving 50 strokes each time, and my back shows the marks. I was flogged over the hands several times. This was before I understood the ways of the place, and to make myself understood by them; latterly, they have treated me well. I have within the last 8 months forwarded three petitions to the Governor of Loanda, through the Governor of Benguella, but have received no reply. I stated I had committed no crime and asked to be allowed to return to my country."

Signed, JOSEPH HARDY.

I immediately turned back to the Governor's house, taking Hardy with me. I told His Excellency the story that I had heard, and that although it appeared to me the man was a Liberian, and not a British subject, still his case was a very hard one, if true. I expressed my readiness to take the man on board the *Torch*, if he was allowed to leave at once: if he was not, I should consider it my duty to represent the case to the Authorities at Loanda. The Governor after examining the office records said he could find no reason for detaining Hardy, if I would take him. He was sent to Benguella, he said, because he had been found as a vagrant at St. Paul's, so without passing any forms whatever, Hardy was handed over to me, and expressing my thanks, I took him on board the *Torch* and entered him as a Krooman. He was a superior style of man to what Kroomen are generally. Spoke grammatical English, could write, and was a fair sailor and cooper. On further enquiry at St. Paul's I found his story to be substantially true. It is not unlikely that he touched it up with a little colour, but it is a fact that the man had been 22 months in prison, for some time in chains, and had been flogged (for the marks were visible), for no greater crime than vagrancy.

While on this subject I may mention, that having at one time gained possession of a native who had robbed one of our merchants at a trading station near the Congo, I conferred with the merchant as to the manner of punishing the thief. He replied "Oh ! give him to me, I'll flog him and then get the Governor of Loanda to pack him off to St. Thomas for life." The place where the merchant resided was at some distance from the Portuguese province. A planter, Portuguese, also told me he punished his labourers by riveting their hands together and sending them to Benguella, with a note to the Governor to request that the culprit might be properly flogged !

I mention these anecdotes to show the manner in which justice is administered in Africa by the Portuguese.

While at Benguella several natives spoke to us in English. They had been slaves released by our men-of-war, and landed at St. Helena, where they learnt our language.

We arrived at St. Paul's again on the 2nd November. Rain had fallen, and the drooping trees that shaded the streets lifted up their heads. Some accacias were one mass of lovely scarlet bloom.

The civil war was over for the season ! The rains had obliged the Portuguese to retire from the open country. These ex-convicts don't see the fun of fighting—even a " nigger." Food was at such a price that slaves were to be had for the asking, and without doubt it went hard with the old and infirm.

We stayed only a few hours at St. Paul's and sailed for Kinsembo, where we anchored at 1 p.m. the next day. The English factories, five or six in number, are built on a red bluff close to the sea—a very healthy situation. It is only a few miles north of Ambriz, the Portuguese frontier town. Its business is principally in ivory, and in selling European goods to Portuguese, who smuggle them into Angola. Two large caravans of ivory had just come down from the interior and there was considerable excitement, as trade goods enough to purchase were not in stock. The clerks in charge of factories, here as elsewhere, appeared very young, but full of zeal. I could only stay a few hours, but the country is very pretty, no thick jungle, but undulating prairie land interspersed with trees. High land in the back ground. Cattle do well, and a good beast can always be obtained for £4 or £5.

The next morning we reached Ambrizette. The factories raised a great display of bunting in our honour.

As another instance of Coast justice, I relate a circumstance brought to my notice here.

Some of our young factors played a practical joke on a Portuguese clerk. He took it into his head that he had discovered the perpetrator, he seized a sword and made a murderous attack upon Mr. Moffat, whom he seriously wounded in the head. A German gentleman interfered, and was wounded in the hand. Another gentleman disarmed the Portuguese and quieted him. Mr. Moffat demanded an apology and £50 damages from the Portuguese, who immediately appealed to the Native Queen of Ambrizette for protection, and it was said offered her all the goods in his store, if she would save his life. The Queen, at any rate, sent a body of men

K

who removed the Portuguese, and the store was claimed by another merchant as having been bought by him. Mr. Moffat then seized a surf boat, which belonged to his assailant, and kept it.

This is the kind of manner in which disputes are obliged to be settled in a country where there is a large trade, but no constituted authority to enforce law. As for native law it is open for purchase to the highest bidder.

I went over the factories here again. One merchant showed me 31 large elephants' tusks, the trade of the two previous days. This gentleman told me his average sale of rum was a pipe—over 100 gallons—a day. He has seen a native drink a pint of this stuff, raw, without taking his lips from the bottle. I saw a native leave this store wearing a scarlet tunic with yellow facings, and the number "17" on the shoulder strap.

The gunpowder is kept in small white-washed magazines at some distance from the factories. I noticed they were locked with "puzzle padlocks," those which require a certain number of letters to be brought in line before they will open. My informant told me that these padlocks were the only ones that the natives could not pick.

I heard the particulars of a case of piracy which had occurred on this Coast a few months previously, and I received directions from England to endeavour to bring the offenders to justice. They were most likely living near Kabenda.

On the 7th I returned to the Congo. I had asked the merchants to prepare some suggestions, by which piracy in this river could be stopped without constant recourse to fire and sword.

I found they had none to offer, so I made an attempt to do something without them. I called on the Chiefs to hold a friendly palaver. Unfortunately, I had been detained two days longer than I meant, waiting for the mail steamer to reach Ambrizette. I found that some of the Chiefs of the Northern bank had come to Banana on the 5th to see me. As I had not kept my tryst, I asked if it would be safe for me to go to their towns to see them. The merchants thought it would, if I did not go in a man-of-war's boat or with arms, and if I was accompanied by interpreters and trade friends. Mr. Burney kindly placed his boat and Kroomen at our disposal. Accompanied by Lieutenant-Commander Larcom, of the *Pioneer*, Mr. Burney, and some other gentlemen, a native interpreter, and hammock bearers, we started for Nemlao's town. We landed safely, and went a few yards into the bush, until we reached a clearance. When we were getting into our hammocks, a party of natives came rushing down the path towards us, gesticulating wildly, and pointing guns at us in a menacing manner. The leader was known to our interpreter as Killio, headman to King Nemlao. He said

K 2

we should not go one step further, and if we did not
return to our boat he would fire. We explained our
object was a friendly palaver; that we had no arms
with us, and it was plain we did not come to fight.
He replied that Sunday was the proper day for a
white man to pay friendly visits, and this was not
Sunday. We said that after this insult we should
return to our boats, but our object had been to make
friendly arrangements with Nemlao, and we should
not come to him on such a message again, if he allowed
us to be insulted. The King's brother George then
appeared on the scene, and throwing himself at our feet
besought us not to return, but to proceed on our
mission and see the King. I refused to do so unless
the armed men were removed and the King came
to where I was. A row then began between George
and Killio, and the excitement was intense. More
armed men filled the bush. Mr. Burney's native
interpreter behaved with great pluck, going straight up
to Killio's gun, which was pointed at him, and turning
the muzzle up towards the sky. Our boat got aground
in trying to get off, and for some minutes we were sub-
jected to volleys of abuse from Killio, and had about
50 guns pointing at us. Afterwards we learnt that
Killio's great excitement was caused by one of our
party having, as he believed, an " evil eye" or " bad
fetish," as he expressed it. Whatever was the cause,
we certainly did not believe at one time that the

affair would end without bloodshed. I was thankful that it did, my object being to bring about a peaceful arrangement for the safe navigation of the Congo, and not to complicate matters by fresh deeds of violence, but savages are not civilized in a day. These Congo men have perhaps the worst repute on the Coast. It is the result of the old slave trade. The sole occupation of these tribes used to be in connection with it, and as they don't like the labour which legitimate traffic entails, they find piracy a pleasant compromise.

Finding we had a treaty with King Antonio, who lived on the South bank, near Shark's Point, we obtained a pilot who could take the *Pioneer* to his town. This King has the greatest power on the river, and in 1865 a treaty had been made with his predecessor on the " stool," for the abolition of the slave trade, and the suppression of river piracy. In consideration of a yearly " dash" he was bound to discover the perpetrators of piratical attacks on British vessels, and to aid British officers by information, and his authority, in bringing them to justice.

No ship had ever been to Antonio's town before. Our pilot had been to it in a canoe, but he had only taken a vessel of any larger size—a slaver I am afraid —within three miles of it. The passage was through a mangrove swamp, the channel deep, after the bar was crossed. As we drew near the town, other trees were visible, the ground began to rise in undulations, and

patches of well-cultivated land were frequent, but the
people were in a great fright, and ran into the bush as
fast as they could.   "King Peter," of Banana, Mr.
Burney's interpreter, who behaved so well the previous
day, was sure we should never see Antonio.   "No,
no," he repeated, "King lib for bush."   But as soon as
we anchored we sent our ambassador on shore with a
small preliminary "dash" and a friendly message, and
we soon saw the people creeping back towards the
water, cautiously peeping round trees at first, but in a
few minutes crowding down to have a good stare at us,
and jabbering like a set of monkeys.   Then a canoe
came off with some of our Shark's Point friends, who
were evidently in high feather with the sense of their
importance.   Our first message from Antonio was
that he was gone "for bush," that is, to the bush, to
make fetish for rain, but soon afterwards our "King
Peter" returned with a message that Antonio would
see us.

Lieutenant-Commander Larcom, and I, and the
Paymaster of the *Pioneer*, with a small black following,
landed, and walked to the King's house.   We found
His Majesty seated in State in the open.   A few
lengths of cotton cloth were fastened up, as a kind of
screen behind him, to which were pinned some very
common pictures.   The King held a crucifix in his
hand.   He had prepared gin cases, covered with
pocket-handkerchiefs, as seats for us.   An umbrella

was held over his head. His suite was not large, and he was the "meanest" King I had seen in West Africa. He had a decanter of water and some tumblers placed before us. We explained the object of our visit. He pretended to know a little about "the book" his predecessors had made with England. He said he had heard there was "a book" but had never seen it. We read him the Articles and explained them.

He said, "What for then you no dash me, as book say?"

"Because your men rob our ships," we replied. We told him that we would sooner pay him "a dash" than burn his towns, but piracy must be stopped. I never saw a native so greedy for a "dash" as this man. Rum, he was very eager for. What we did give was an order for £3, on a factor at Banana, and I am told he was very well pleased at having got so much out of us. Our visit to this out-of-the-way place did much good; and if the lower reach of the Congo and its numerous creeks was surveyed, and an independent Englishman, not a trader, brought in contact with the natives oftener, and their confidence gained, all manner of hindrances to the river trade would soon disappear. The truth is, these tribes deal with small Portuguese traders, and not much with Banana, and a mutual dislike exists between Antonio's people and the Banana traders.

Some of the Kings whose names were attached to the treaty of 1865 had ceased to be known. We did not seek them, but left the news of our interview with Antonio to percolate through the villages and towns by the " native post," which we knew to travel quickly.

Mr. Larcom had noticed that if he went for a walk anywhere on this part of the coast, his movements were quickly made known in every direction ; and if he missed a companion, the first native he met that could speak English would tell him which way he had taken, although he could not have spoken from his own personal knowledge. This system of passing news on from one to the other we called the " native post."

On our return to the *Pioneer* we found a very brisk trade going on. I saw an armful of tobacco bought for two empty bottles. Some good otter skins were produced, and plenty of live stock, and parrots. We saluted King Antonio with two guns ; and the people yelled like jackals in reply.

The return passage was made without any difficulty.

CHAPTER VIII.

At this time, 10th November, we had more fever in the ship than we had at any one time on the coast, but none of the cases were very serious. By taking prompt measures, and moving at once to Kabenda the cases rapidly recovered. The rains were not heavy, but in mid-day the heat was great, for the coast, the thermometer in the shade reaching 88°. But the mornings and evenings were pleasant : and we could always enjoy a walk of four or five miles at these times. European residents seldom take exercise in any part of West Africa, and our proceedings astonished the natives. About Kabenda these short stretches into the country were very interesting. Brighter or more beautiful greens the eye never rested on than in the woods. The orange and lemon trees in blossom filled the air with perfume. The prairie grass was full of wild flowers, and the beautiful plumage of the birds I have already spoken of. The little villages of huts built of split palm stems and thatched with palm leaves, were kept cleanly swept up, surrounded by neat gardens and graceful banana trees. The banana trees are always near the villages so that they may be secure from thieves. The Indian corn and cassada bushes are planted in neat rows, the sweet potatoes and pea nuts in regular beds. In the rear of each dwelling is a small house, raised three or four feet from the ground on posts, to protect it from snakes and vermin. This is for the poultry.

The people were always well clothed, in African fashion, and always civil, Sometimes when we got a little further from the town than usual, the women would run into the bush in fright at meeting us, or braver mothers would bring out their naughty children to show them the horrid white man who had come to take them away! If screams of terror were any indication of the black infants' feelings, I should say they were quite equal to that of any English baby when threatened to be handed over to a wandering Lascar pedlar.

One evening we sat down on a village bench to rest, and asked for palm wine. While it was being brought to us, we delighted the boys, by drawing their likenesses with our walking sticks in the sand. There were roars of laughter as they detected particular features in our rough portraits, and I have seldom seen such enjoyment as our ten minutes artistic performance afforded. The headman of this village took us to his house to show us his treasures. Not his wives! he had four of those he told us, but they lived in little huts by themselves within the cane fence which surrounded his whole premises; but his wealth, his money. This was kept in a room, the sides of which were boarded, and had a door fastened with a good strong padlock. It smelt very musty as we entered, for there was no window, or any means of ventilating it. In the corner were piles of cotton cloth, round the sides dozens of empty bottles, powder barrels and gin cases: several pictures hung against the walls, one of them an engraving of the "Black Brunswicker," well framed; and several guns, flints, brass rods, and coloured bottles and beads were arranged about the room. The old man was very proud of his possessions, and carried the key of his treasure room suspended by an iron chain, of no slight dimensions, round his neck.

At the native burial ground are to be seen graves ornamented with wooden crosses, having on them an imitation of our letters: the graves are also covered with pieces of glass and crockery, sometimes broken and sometimes not. I noticed this also near Antonio's town and elswhere. The graves are also sometimes railed round. In the centre of the town of Kabenda is a wooden cross painted black, on which is printed the Lord's prayer in Portuguese. There are no missionaries in the place and have not been for many years, but there was a house called a school house where children were taught something, I was told, but I don't know what. The schoolmaster was a native. Flags were

always flown on Sundays, people put on their best
clothes, and did very little work ; but these were the
only outward sign of any other religion than fetishism
to be seen. The fetish man had great power. No one
would think of robbing an orange or banana tree about
which he had hung a few charms, and he could always
discover a witch or a wizard. The ordeal by poison was
often had recourse to, to discover thieves, and the fetish
man administered the dose. It was called Sassa water.
If the accused drank the poison and died, he was
guilty ; if he vomited it, he was innocent. We were
told that the fetish man could always be " got at," by
a sufficient bribe from a suspected person, and the
strength of the mixture would be so reduced as to be
innocuous. If one person challenges another to undergo
the ordeal, as a proof that he is not guilty of an
offence charged against him, that other is bound to
accept it ; but, if he survives, the challenger has to
pay damages and give a feast to the relatives of the
accused. A feast of this kind took place during our
stay at Kabenda, and some of our officers went to it.
There was dancing and horn-blowing, clapping of hands,
and such like entertainment, but nothing that could be
called by us—amusement.

Francisco Franco, commonly called " Chico Franco,"
was Chief of Kabenda. The great King was some
mysterious individual, said to live in the far interior,
whose " fetish" forbad his looking upon the sea or upon

a white man. Chico Franco and his brothers had all
made a good deal of money in the good old slaving
days. They were now old, and very honest !

The Chief's right hand man, minister, or whatever
he might call him, was Capita. He judged Kabenda ;
and it was amusing to see him at his magisterial work,
seated in front of his house, with a circle of litigants
before him to whom he meted out justice in the most
approved fashion. Offenders, of crimes of a serious
nature, were punished by fine or imprisonment; the
latter is technically termed " tying up," and I saw one
or two men " tied up" by a chain to a post near his
premises. These people are provided with a code of
laws of their own ; not written, but well understood,
and it must not be thought that they are without
morals. In certain cases, adultery is punished with
death. A man may have as many wives as he likes,
but he must pay for them to their parents, and be
married according to native customs. A wife costs
from £5 to £20 according to her family, for there are
many steps in the social scale in this country. As the
wife has to provide the family with food, till the ground,
and keep the house in order, she helps her husband to
get more wives as soon as he can afford it, to help her
in her work !

But it is unlawful for one man to take another's
wife.

I heard of a case in Kabenda where high treason

had been punished by roasting alive. Chico Franco
kept some of his wealth in boxes under his bed. His
sons bribed a servant to procure the key of the box,
and they took doubloons from it occasionally.

Chico Franco discovered their dishonesty, and finding that the sons had obtained the key of the box from
his steward he had him roasted on the beach.

At about two miles from Kabenda lives the Baron
Punha, a Portuguese nobleman and Colonel in the
Angola Militia; but he is a pure native, as black as a
coal. He gained his honours in the slave trade, through
the influence of some Governor-General of Angola, and
he is reported to have gained a nice fortune at the same
time.

And now I discovered that the perpetrators of the
ivory robbery from Ambrizette were actually living
near Kabenda, and that the ivory had been landed close
to. I wrote a very strong letter to Chico Franco, de-
manding that the "Padron" of the boat at least should
be handed over to me, with what ivory could be found.
After a good deal of pressing the man was sent, with
four tusks bearing Mr. Stuart's private mark. I at
at once took the man to Ambrizette, and assembled a
Naval court to try him. The charge was that he had
been sent from Maculla, a place a few miles north of
Ambrizette, to the latter port, with 50 tusks of ivory.
Instead of going to Ambrizette, however, he ran the
boat to the north, crossed the Congo stream, beached

the boat near Kabenda, and made off with the ivory. His story was that his boat was leaky, that he was taking her to the nearest port for repairs, when she sank, and the crew were drowned except himself and another man. The evidence showed this to be impossible; the man was found guilty, and sentenced to six months' imprisonment. He was kept on board the *Torch* until an opportunity arose of sending him to the Cape or St. Helena prison. He got quite at home on board the ship, and liked to be allowed to make himself useful, at pumping, or trimming coals; but he said he never could return to his own country again, as he had said at his trial Chico Franco had " told a lie." One night we were at anchor in the Congo stream, two miles from shore, and the current running out to sea at the rate of four miles an hour, when the prisoner jumped overboard, and was never more heard of. Without doubt he was drowned.

Another occurrence took place at this time illustrative of the various matters our naval officers on this coast have to attend to. A Portuguese trader at Chiloango had been brutally murdered by his servants. It was said he was a very cruel man, and his fate did not surprise anyone, but this is not to the matter; he left many debts and some property. His creditors had a meeting and agreed to bring in his goods from the out stations to the main factory, and having ascertained their value and the total amount of his debts, to divide them equitably among the creditors. A Portuguese creditor at Chiloango offered to convey the goods at that station to Black point, the main factory, in two schooners of his own, and the goods were embarked; but as there was no chance of the deceased debtor's estate paying twenty shillings in the pound, this cunning Portuguese ordered his vessels to make away as fast as they could for Ambriz in Portuguese territory, where he knew he would be able to manage affairs so as to cover his debt in full. Unfortunately for him, an English creditor had a steamer at Black point, and hearing of the treachery of their Portuguese fellow creditor, the others convened a meeting and commissioned the English steamer to proceed in chase of the schooners and bring them back. The schooners were found, and towed into Kabenda. They had Portuguese colours flying and correct Portuguese papers. The English creditors came to me to ask me to unload the schooners and place the cargo under seal on shore. I pointed out that I had no power to take such a course, and they had no power to seize a foreign ship on the high seas, although it was plain in equity she was committing an illegal act. I offered to go to Loanda at once and place the matter in our Consul's hands, but the merchants said they should consider their debt entirely lost if the goods ever got within Portuguese jurisdiction; and one of these gentlemen was interested to the extent of £4000. I therefore refused to interfere with the schooners at all, unless a charge of piracy, on oath was made against them ; and on my telling the merchants that they would have to answer for any charge of illegal capture that the Portuguese might make, and we were then in neutral waters, I told them to follow the custom and law of the country. The schooners subsequently sailed back to Black point, and I have no doubt the goods were unloaded.

A Portuguese man-of-war arrived at Kabenda that evening, and when I told him what had taken place he only expressed surprise that I had'nt seized the schooners, saying " all these traders are ' degredados,' and don't deserve protection, and anyone can get Portuguese papers, and hoist our colours."

Considering the large amount of trade being done on the South Coast, and the absence of all constituted authority between Gaboon and Ambriz, it is wonderful how any semblance of law is maintained. Some rough justice does take place now and then as may be imagined.

On the 2nd December Commodore Commerell arrived in the *Rattlesnake*, and on the 4th he came on board the *Torch* for the purpose of ascending the Congo.

The only pilot we could obtain at Banana had not been up the river for three months, and he found that the channel had filled up, which he had been accustomed to use. When we were three miles below Punta de

L

Lenha we were obliged to anchor. This was 30 miles above Banana, and the channel had been wide and deep so far. The river was very wide at this point, but shoal places were visible in every direction. We prepared the steam pinnace to go to M'Boma next day. The stream was very rapid. Heavy showers of rain fell and large floating islands passed us. The river banks were still covered with mangrove, the first palm tree being met at Punta de Lenha.

At daylight next morning we started. In an hour we reached the factories. We found deep water close to the bushes on the northern bank. Everyone and everything looked miserable at Punta de Lenha. The river had risen to within a few inches of the floors of the factories. Alligators had invaded the yards and stolen the pigs. Trade was at a stand still. About the only thing to be noticed at this place besides its misery, was the large bed of dead oyster shells among the mangroves close to. They are used to make a hard wharf for landing stores on, by ramming them down between piles.

A mile above Punta de Lenha the current was so strong our boat could hardly creep round the points, although she was steaming 7 knots an hour. We kept our course as close as possible to the banks. The river widened out into an expanse at least 12 miles wide and covered with low islands. The rain fell in torrents until 2 p.m., when we found ourselves approaching a different kind of the country, and the sun bursting out showed us as fine a bit of river scenery as could be wished for. The mangroves had disappeared. Scattered palms had taken their place, Cliffs of red sandstone came down to the river, and in the back-ground were green hills and distant mountains. The dark brown river looked well in this setting. In the centre it was disturbed by small whirlpools, and the sea breeze raised its waves.

We reached M'Boma at 4 p.m. The Delta was passed and the river concentrated into one stream, about a mile wide, and at a little distance from either shore 50 fathoms deep.

We were most hospitably received by Mr. de Jongh of the Dutch house at Banana. All the Banana houses were represented at M'Boma, and small steamers and schooners plied between the two places conveying the goods. This was a dull time of the year. The floods prevented people crossing the streams up country; and the river was running too swiftly for canoes to return against stream without great trouble.

M'Boma used to be the great slave market for slaves on the South Coast, as Lagos was in the "Bights." Thousands used to be kept on hand in baracoons, for intending shippers to buy, and they used either be to sent in canoes down the river or marched across country to meet a vessel ready to leave the Coast. We were told it was not uncommon to have

30,000 slaves in stock, and the number seldom fell below 10,000.

Of course M'Boma has sunk in importance since the slave trade ceased, but it is rapidly beginning to revive, as trade increases. It is expected that the ivory caravans will soon come here instead of going to Angolo. As it is, a large quantity of palm oil, pea nuts, and wax are brought to this market, and small quantities of every commodity known in the African market.

Mr. de Jongh's board groaned with plenty; and he had most comfortable rooms and beds for us to sleep in. He told us he found M'Boma the healthiest station on the river, but that it would be still pleasanter farther up. The falls of Yellala which interrupt navigation 40 miles from M'Boma had not been visited by any person at that station, and the accounts known of them here were mythical. Some stated them to be mere rapids, others high falls plainly to be heard at five miles distance. The natives from Yellala were said to object to white men going into their country, but there is no doubt that white men will soon go there; already they were establishing factories twenty miles nearer the falls, and these we proposed visiting.

There was no thick bush visible near M'Boma. The country consisted of high prairie land, interspersed with clumps of trees. This may be said to be the general character of the coast between Ambriz and the third degree of south latitude except at the mouths of rivers where the mangrove swamps are. The soil is rich and cultivation easy. Some of the trees are of great size, and the wood is both useful and ornamental. Cattle, sheep, and poultry will do well; but the people have not yet learnt either agricultural or pastoral farming.

We learnt something more of Coast justice at M'Boma. We saw five men chained together with iron rings round their necks, as in Angola. We ascertained they were being punished for pilfering. "And" added our informant, " I am very lenient to them, my neighbour there would tie them head and feet together and throw them into the river!"

" But," we asked, " do not the native Chiefs complain of this ?"

" Oh ! no" was the reply, " they would if blood was shed, we should then have to pay blood-money."

I had previously heard many stories from our traders of the manner they punished native offenders, and I knew they were guided by native customs. I had never heard anything so bad as this. I am glad to say in this instance the person spoken of was no countryman of ours. But I heard afterwards that in another place an Englishman had thus punished natives for stealing. The only punishment I ever witnessed natives undergoing from our traders was "tying up" for debt; but I have heard them speak of flogging them, and have heard of worse things from others.

Mr. de Jongh told us there was a village near M'Boma, which was a kind of monastery. All males of the tribes in the neighbourhood went there for a short period of their lives, some remaining two years. During this time they never washed, kept apart from their wives, and wore a peculiar dress. As long as they did this they were maintained at the public expense. All males of these tribes are circumcised.

There are seven kings at M'Boma. They used to be powerful men in former days, but their glory has departed with the slave trade.

We saw Captain Burton's name cut on a cotton tree near the Dutch factory.

After a pleasant night's rest, and a refreshing breakfast. we started at early morning up stream. Some of our M'Boma friends accompanied us. The current was so strong we could make little way, and after we had gone five miles, our coals began to give out and we were obliged to return. This was very disappointing, as at every mile the scenery became more lovely and interesting. We all pronounced it a noble and beautiful river and prophesied a great future for it.

We went down stream fast enough, and after making a short stay at M'Boma and lunching at Punta de Lenha, we reached the *Torch* early in the afternoon, and the *Rattlesnake* off Banana before sunset.

Shortly after this we left the South Coast, with the

Commodore, for the " Bights," and on the 17th December anchored off the fairway buoy of the Bonny.

The Bonny is one of the many mouths of the Niger. It is wide and deep within its bar, but shoals run out to seawards for many miles, and the fair-way buoy is nearly ten miles from its entrance. The tides run strongly in and out.

The object of the Commodore's visit was to arrange a peace between the Bonny and Opobo men. In consequence of a war which these people kept up, without any prospect of a conclusion, trade was nearly ruined.

The position of affairs was this :—

George Pepple is nominally King of Bonny. He is a young man; has been educated in England; speaks excellent English, and is well informed. He receives a large "comey," or export duty, on oil, and trades as well. His Chiefs, however, have more real power, and more wealth than he has. A few years previous to this, two of the principal ones grew very jealous of each other, and gathering factions round them, fought their quarrel out in Bonny town. These men, Oko Jumbo and Ja-ja, pretty fairly divided Bonny sympathy between them, and the patronage of the foreign merchants. But at this first struggle the fates were against Ja-ja. At last, by the assistance of white traders, he was able to escape from Bonny together with his followers, and he established himself at a river named the Opobo, another branch of the Niger, forty miles east of the Bonny. This river has internal communication with the Bonny. By the aid of his white friends, Ja-ja quickly supplied himself with artillery, armed heavy war canoes, and erected batteries in positions where he was able to stop oil going down to Bonny from the inland markets. Ja-ja also declared himself independent of Pepple, and to be King of Opobo. The Bonnymen had their backers also, but they were unable to break Ja-ja's blockade. However, they discovered another passage higher up the stream, through which light canoes could pass, and here the Bonnymen established batteries, which prevented all trade coming down. Ja-ja was unable to break this blockade, and thus trade came to a standstill.

The war was called Oko Jumbo's and Ja-Ja's war as it really was, Pepple being a mere puppet. There is, however, considerable respect paid to family in Bonny, and Pepple's family was good. Oko Jumbo's or Ja-Ja's nothing to speak of.

Oko Jumbo told us he had 80 war canoes armed with cannon, and Ja-Ja said he had 100. Besides, they had a large number of guns in their batteries. The guns in the latter were not mounted on carriages—these were not approved of,—but were laid on the ground with their muzzles resting on fallen trunks of trees at different angles. The cannon were of every possible pattern and description.

No general action ever took place between the

contending parties. For two or three years they stood their ground, neither party gaining or losing. Skirmishes took place of the outposts. Stragglers were caught on either side, killed and eaten; but the end seemed as far off as ever. At length our Foreign Office determined to interfere, and Commodore Commerell and Consul Livingstone were instructed to open the river for trade.

The Consul met the Commodore at the Bonny, and they at once held a preliminary palaver with Pepple and his Chiefs on board the *Torch.*

King George wore a grey tweed suit and a seal-skin cap; but Oko Jumbo and Ada Alison, his Chiefs, wore the native dress.

The King's address was very grandiloquent; he talked of referring the question between himself and the rebel Ja-Ja to arbitration of some neutral native King, who understood African customs, in the same manner as we had submitted our difference with America to arbitration.

He refused to meet Ja-Ja at all, and heaped abuse on him, but he was told that neither he nor Ja-Ja would be allowed to ruin a fine trade any more, and if necessary he must meet Ja-Ja.

Bonny Town is in a most unhealthy situation amidst a mangrove swamp. The houses are built of clay and roofed with corrugated iron. Oko Jumbo's house is a two-storied building of some pretension.

The white traders live on board large airy hulks in the river. These vessels are roofed over and comfortably fitted up, and are more pleasant to live in than any place on shore would be.

We visited the Ju-Ju house. This is the only religious building, set apart for pagan worship, I have seen in Africa. It is a small building roofed with iron, of one room, containing the skulls and other parts of human victims killed in sacrifice. It has also in it a number of goats' skulls, and a large stuffed lizard was in a recess of a square pillar of bones and skulls standing in the centre of the apartment. In front of this is a hole in the floor to receive the blood and libations of wine offered to the Gods. I could not learn exactly what ceremonies took place here. The natives did not like talking of them. Human sacrifices and cannibal feasts do occur occasionally, but the victims are killed at the river side.

I was told the bodies were then taken to the Ju-Ju house to be cut up by the "Fetish" men, who reserved the hands and feet for themselves, and served out the other portions to the persons wishing to partake of the feast. The flesh was boiled and eaten with yams.

There is a missionary station close to Bonny Town, and I have no doubt the missionaries are striving hard to stop the savage practices of the natives, but it is more than the Chiefs are able to do to stop these old customs suddenly, and consequently missionaries and other Whites must be patient. The practice of cannibalism is less common every year, as is also human sacrifice.

A Bonny canoe is a large-sized boat, sometimes paddled by as many as 24 men, who use very short paddles. The canoes are hollowed out of a single tree, and very well shaped.

The men sing as they paddle and make a great noise. When there is any wind they use a sail.

The trade of the river in peaceful times is very great, it consists almost entirely in palm oil, which is brought from distant native markets in these large canoes. The natives are very jealous of white men going direct to these markets in the interior, and as yet they have seldom been visited.

From the Bonny the Commodore and Consul went to the Opobo with the *Rattlesnake* and *Torch.*

Commodore Commerell and Consul Livingstone proceeded up the Opobo in the *Torch.* The country is all mangrove swamp. The town, of the usual native style, in an unhealthy situation. Several trading hulks were moored off it.

Ja-Ja came on board, attended by his Secretary, a Sierra Leone man, who spoke good English. Ja-Ja's English was the usual Coast " patter." The Chief was dressed in native, his Secretary in European style.

Ja-Ja seemed anxious to make peace, but said he had sworn his great oath never to cross the Opobo bar again, and therefore would not go to Bonny. He agreed to meet the Bonnymen, on board one of our ships, inside the Opobo bar, and submit the quarrel to the arbitration of the Commodore and Consul, with the Chiefs of New Calabar for assessors.

Before parting we fired a large rocket for Ja-Ja's entertainment.

The Commodore then returned to Bonny, and sent us to Fernando Po for coal, and to order the *Supply* to Opobo.

We returned on Christmas morning with the only bullocks we could obtain for the squadron. But no ships were there, so we had the beef to ourselves.

We had a broiling hot day, and spent it, side by side, with the *Supply*, seeing which could roll the heaviest.

The day after, orders reached us by the *Coquette* to go to Bonny and prepare to embark the King and Chiefs for Opobo.

As we were at the point of sailing from Bonny, a fire broke out in the town which quickly destroyed one-third of it. This was Ada Alison's portion. We went on shore, and found the poor old man in great grief, but bearing up stoically. His women were weeping and screaming near his house, and one of them rushed into the river to drown herself, saying that life was not worth having now her property was all destroyed. Very likely the said property consisted of a few iron rings and glass beads worth two shillings. She was saved, and on second thoughts, consented to live. Of course there was no getting the Chiefs on board for that day.

But the next morning King George, with his brother, Prince Charles, Oko-Jumbo, Prime Minister, Ada Alison, and Captain Hart, Councillors Waripoo, Commander-in-Chief, John Jumbo, and several other influential men and chiefs of the Bonny tribe, with some Okreeka Chiefs, who were to act as assessors for the Bonnymen embarked.

With their attendants they numbered 39. They brought as much luggage with them as if they were going to England. Not in mats or bundles, but in Russia leather portmanteaux and japanned tin cases, and French valises.

All the head men were in European costume and some of them well-dressed. George wore an Indian pith helmet, a black frock coat, and London-made nether garments. A heavy gold watch chain ornamented his waistcoat. But some of the Chiefs were evidently uncomfortable, and light leather shoes were soon replaced by carpet slippers. They had to live under the awning on deck as I had no accommodation for them below. The Chiefs did not give much trouble, but King George thought himself deserving extra attention, which I could not give him. They were supplied with a plentiful table, but a limit was obliged

to be put to the wine and beer. Rum, they did not
consider "gentleman's drink." Old Waripoo was constantly coming to me to shake hands and say, "Cap'n,
my belly cold," by which I knew he wanted brandy.
I must say though I never saw any of them take too
much : some of the young fellows gave themselves great
airs.   I thought John Jumbo, who has recently joined
our expedition on the Gold Coast, the best of them.

There was some trouble in getting the Bonny men
to cross the Opobo bar.   The *Pioneer* went up to
Ja-Ja's town with the Commodore and the New
Calabar Chiefs, who had come in the *Rattlesnake* with
him.   These latter were fine specimens of natives.   The
King wore a long black silk gown, a tall "Lincoln and
Bennett" hat, and patent leather boots, with a massive
silver collar round his neck.   His chiefs wore silk
dresses and "gum" boots.

The Bonny men were told they might go in the
Pioneer if they liked, but they were not to show
themselves on deck when Ja-Ja came on board.   Their
curiosity overcame their scruples, and they all went.

As soon as the time of palaver was arranged the
Pioneer returned outside the bar.

The next morning, early, the Bonny men made a
grand toilet.   Oko-Jumbo wore a tall white hat in a
jaunty style, and King George had rivals as leaders of
fashion.   There were no fancy costumes, no uniforms,
but none of the chiefs wore the native dress.

Ja-Ja came off to meet the *Pioneer* in a naval uniform, with a military staff-officer's cocked hat, but when he saw our party he felt rather ashamed of himself and appeared in a plainer, although an equally expensive dress afterwards.

The Palaver lasted for three days. George spoke well for his cause, and his arguments were good. The Assessors listened attentively, and the King of New Calabar expressed his opinion of the case clearly and sensibly. It was only possible to settle such a dispute by a compromise. Both parties had done much harm to each other, but neither was strong enough to conquer the other. An arrangement was then made that the markets should be divided! the Bonny men to trade with certain ones named, and the Opobo with certain others. On this basis peace was at length agreed upon, and a treaty to that effect was made and sworn to by the native oath, which was to the following effect.

" Listen hearts and souls of Bonny, Opobo, Calabar, and Okreeka.

"May the God of the Sun,
May the God of the Moon,
May the God of the Earth,
May the God of the Sea,
May the God of the Sky,

destroy me ; may my bones rot in my body before I die ; and may slaves eat my flesh, if I, Ja-Ja, fail to keep this ju-ju with thee, Oko Jumbo."

Then a portion of a glass of wine was spilled on the ground, and the rest of it drank.

The Bonny men pretended at first to be ill satisfied with the terms they had obtained, but after a little while they owned that peace, at any price, was a blessing to them, as the trade was leaving the river in consequence of the war.

During the palaver days the weather had fortunately kept fine, but as we were on our return to Bonny the rain fell in torrents. It was night time, and I felt for the poor fellows on deck and their fine clothes. It was pitch dark, so they could not be seen; as day dawned, I found them all reduced to a clout, smoking their pipes, and looking the picture of happiness! The weather got fine enough for them to land in full feather, and we were not at all sorry to be rid of the cumberers of our deck for the previous five days.

We were also glad to receive our orders to proceed to Gibraltar. The *Supply* had been on shore, and we were to convoy her to Cadiz, first going to Ascension with the *Coquette*, whose crew were suffering severely from fever. She had 37 cases among her crew of 57 men. The *Supply* and *Coquette* had been sent to Anno Bom to get fresh stock, and await for us.

We parted company with the Commodore on the 6th January, and on the 8th anchored off Anno Bom, where we found our consorts waiting for us.

CHAPTER IX.

ANNO BOM is situated 2° South of the Equator. It nominally belongs to Spain, as a dependency of Fernando Po, but there is no Spanish official on the island. No tax or tribute of any kind is paid by the people, no Spanish flag is flown, and a Spanish man-of-war is seldom seen there. There is no white man living on the island, and the inhabitants speak Portuguese. American whale ships call occasionally for wood and water, and a few of the people spoke English. Their account of themselves is that they are the descendants of a cargo of slaves wrecked on the island more than 100 years ago,

There are about 600 people on the island, all living in one town at its north end.

The island is high, and volcanic in its formation. It is covered with vegetation from the sea to the summit, and has a most refreshing look. But we were told that within the memory of living men, there had been two years without rain, when all vegetation died, and most of the people died of starvation. The island then looked like a cinder heap. As a rule, however,

M

luxuriant crops are grown, although the soil is shallow and the people bad farmers.

The most noticeable thing in the island is the number of churches. The people profess to be Roman Catholics. A man, wearing a blue blouse and a red handkerchief round his head, came to call upon me, to bid me welcome, and asked for a "dash" of candles. He told me that there were twenty-two churches on the island and several priests, and that he was the Bishop. I never saw any of the others who claimed the clerical office. The Schoolmaster showed me a torn missal, out of which he said he taught the children, and that was the only book I saw. The churches stood all round the town. They were built like the other houses, of boards, and thatched with palm leaves. The largest one, the Cathedral, was the only one I saw used. It has an Altar, with a crucifix on it, and a side chapel with the image of the Virgin. An oil lamp burnt before it. The floor was earthen, and the dead were buried beneath it. A large cross was erected before the door, and at every exit from the town was a cross and a chapel. From the enquiries I made, I found that the people were grossly superstitious, and their religion was strongly impregnated with fetishism.

King David Carter governs the island. He also visited me, to ask for a "dash." When I offered him some rum, as refreshment, he freely helped himself and his interpreter, Tom Bolan, and then put the bottle in his pocket! Then he said it was warm, and asked for a handkerchief, which he also pocketed, and then Tom wanted a handkerchief, which I gave, but told him it was time for him to withdraw, as I saw his object was not to welcome me, but to get what he could from me. In leaving the ship I was greatly amused at Tom Bolan throwing the bottle of rum the King had given him into the water, for a canoe to pick up, as he was afraid of not carrying it safely down the ship's side. It sank!

The people were very dirty and untidy in their dwellings, compared to the Continentals. They were anxious to trade poultry, eggs, and fruit, for biscuit, clothing, and, of course, rum, if they could get it. We had none for them; but it was a fine opportunity for getting rid of old clothes before leaving the Coast.

Besides fowls, the only live stock on the island appeared to be a few pigs and goats. The vegetables were sweet potatoes and yams. They said that they used to grow very large cabbages, but they were out of seed. They were evidently a lazy people, and preferred living upon what grew of itself, with little or no cultivation, such as cassada, sweet potatoes, and bananas. There were pine-apples, oranges, limes, and wild plums in plenty.

Tom Bolan and Alexander Smith had served in American whale ships. They had been to the States, and had learnt shrewdness in that country. These

M 2

worthies acted as our guides to a mountain lake, which lays in the hollow of the old crater, 1,500 feet above the sea.   It was a stiff climb up a slippery path to it, but quite worth the trouble.   The view and scenery were lovely.

The people seemed to suffer a great deal from skin diseases.   The population has ceased to increase, so Bolan said, and there is often great mortality among the children.   There are no vessels on the island large enough to sail to the main land, or the neighbouring Island of St. Thomas.

Anno Bom would apparently make a splendid coffee growing estate.

In one way, at any rate, Anno Bom is an earthly paradise.   Money has no value !   A packet of needles, or a hank of thread, would obtain us two or three pine apples.   A sovereign, nothing !   Even an old bottle or worn-out stockings were better to take to market than dollars !   I actually saw money refused on more than one occasion, and on one of these it was a " dash."

The visit of our three ships was a great god-send to the inhabitants.   We did not find things cheap, compared to the Kabenda tarif.

The climate seemed good, and we were at the Island in the rainy season, when it would be at its worst.

We only remained one day.   The *Coquette's* people were recovering rapidly owing to the change.   There is nothing like immediate change of climate to kill African fever.

We had heavy rains for a few days after leaving, and then a lovely climate in the South East trades until we reached Ascension which we did on the 21st January. The *Coquette* had then only ten fever cases remaining, and they were landed as soon as possible and sent to the commodious hospital which is always kept in readiness.

Ascension is like a huge heap of ashes rising out of the sea. On its summit, at 2000 feet above the sea, where the ocean mists gather, is a little vegetation. Gardens have been established there to provide vegetables for the garrison, and grass enough grows to feed some oxen and sheep for their use. A regular supply of these animals is sent from the Cape of Good Hope.

The island is kept as if it were a ship. A Naval Captain governs it, and its inhabitants are all seamen, marines, and their families. Not an event happens on the island without the Captain's permission. I was even surprised to find that babies could not come into the world without his approval. At least, I saw an official document from the Surgeon reporting the advent of a little stranger, on which the Captain wrote " Approved.—J.B.C."

I thought that the officials on the Gold Coast were the greatest pluralists in the world, but the Captain of Ascension is greater.

He is Captain of a ship of war, Superintendent of the Dockyard, Governor of the island, Sole Legislator, Chief Executive, Coroner, Public prosecutor, Chief Gaoler, and President ex-officio of all local societies, of the Canteen, the Library and the Cricket Club.

The mail steamers call here twice a month, on their homeward voyage from the Cape, so that the letters from England go first to St. Helena and return.

The staple product of the island is turtle. A considerable number of these animals are caught every year and issued as rations to the people on the island, or sent down to the ships on the coast as opportunities offer.

Some of them obtain a great size, weighing as much as 5 cwt. each.

There is a bird very like a seagull which resorts to the island to breed. It is called the " Wide-awake," from its peculiar cry which has that sound. The birds lay their eggs at certain seasons of the year and in one particular place, which is called " Wide-awake Fair," and as many eggs as can be carried can be picked up in an hour or two. They are very good to eat, in size that of a plover's egg, and tasting something like a duck's.

The inhabitants of the island numbered 250, of which 80 were white women and children and 40 African labourers.

As the whole establishment belongs to the Admiralty, the buildings will be understood to be of the same kind as may be seen in any of our Dockyards, and I need not say, that scrupulous order and neatness exists everywhere.

There is a Canteen, where all necessaries, and many luxuries of life can be purchased at a most reasonable figure ; a theatre, a billiard room, a bowling alley, and a skittle ground. There is shooting to be had in the game season, by obtaining a licence from the Governor, for which the charge is a modest half-a-crown. Rabbits, guinea-fowl and partridges are preserved on the " Green Mountain," and wild goats and wild asses are there, if you can get at them and would like to fill your bag with such game. Tradition talks of pheasants, quail, and birds never seen now-a-days, having once been shot.

The climate at the mountain is very pleasant, and a delightful change for men who have been any considerable time on the Coast.

Coaling was a difficult operation at Ascension, owing to the rollers setting in. This is an extraordinary phenomenon. Owing to some unexplained cause, a heavy swell gets up to leeward of Ascension and St. Helena, and breaks against these islands with great force, the wind and swell in the offing being strong in the opposite direction.

We sailed with the " *Supply* " in company, on the 29th January. We had lovely weather across the line, but as soon as we felt the North East trade it got quite cold. In a few days the thermometer fell from 84°, at 8 a.m., to 64°. The wind kept strong against us and we were obliged to call at Dâkar, Cape Verde, for coal. This is in the French province of Senegal, on the mainland, opposite the better known Gorée, which is an island containing a dockyard, barracks, public buildings, and a very considerable town.

Dâkar is a comparatively recent settlement, and much more convenient for trade than Gorée. I am surprised it is not better known. It is a coaling station for the steamers of the " Messageries Maritimes " Company which ply between Bordeaux and Brazil, and French Men of War, bound to Brazil, or round the Cape, coal here also.

An artificial harbour has been formed, inside which ships lay very comfortably and safely. Steamers are coaled expeditiously, and provisions are quickly supplied and the charges moderate.

The natives are a fine race of men, very black, but with regular features; they are Mahomedans; and do not give the French much trouble.

The country around was low and sandy: but by artificial irrigation some well stocked gardens were to be seen; in the season enough cereals were grown for home consumption, and large quantities of pea nuts for exportation. The corn is stored in beehive shaped houses, thatched over, after it has been thrashed out. Wheat, barley, and millet are the kinds used. These people evidently live better than the natives of equatorial Africa.

Several French ladies resided at Dâkar and Gorée, but they went to France in the three very hot months, July, August and September, if possible.

At other times of the year the climate was not at all unpleasant, and at this time—January, it was quite cold at night.

St. Louis, on the river Senegal is the capital of the province where the Governor resides, but the bar of the river is often impassable, and the entrance is always changing. There is a telegraph wire laid between Dâkar and St. Louis, and a telegram reporting the state of the bar is sent to Dâkar every morning. Once the bar is crossed the river is navigable for 500 miles.

A large number of military convicts are employed at the coal depôt, and on the public works.

The coast is very well lighted. The light exhibited on Cape Verde is of the first order, which is necessary, as foggy weather is prevalent and the coast dangerous.

From Dâkar we sailed for Santa Cruz, Teneriffe, thence to Gibraltar, calling at Madeira, and thus we passed along the whole western seaboard of Africa from the Cape of Good Hope to Cape Spartel in the year, calling at most of the places of importance, and gaining such knowledge of the nature of the country and the character of the people as upset many of our pre-conceived ideas.

In the first place, the climate is· not so bad as is generally supposed, except at those places near the mouths of rivers where merchants have located themselves for trading purposes. I hope that it will not be necessary that they should remain in such situations much longer, for trade jealousies with the natives once being overcome, they may be able to move further into the interior, above the mangrove swamps.

In the second place, the soil is capable of producing large quantities of food, of cotton, and other important articles of commerce. Cattle are easily reared. Timber and minerals are abundant, and the latent wealth of the country is enormous.

Thirdly, the coast abounds in good harbours and large rivers, affording natural highways into the interior. The natives, if properly dealt with, soon become friendly, and are easily taught to be useful producers. They are daily becoming greater consumers of European produce.

I had believed otherwise of West Africa; and although I had been on the Coast for a short time, twenty years ago, I had no idea that it was such a magnificent country. I have been to India. I see no reason this country should not have as great a future before it as that.

If the facts mentioned in this book, as they came under my own observation, serve in a small measure to undeceive the English public, who may have formed a similar idea of the country to that I formerly entertained myself, I shall have gained the object I had in view in writing them.

At the same time I do not go to the other extreme, and recommend it as a country for an Englishman to emigrate to. If he should be sent there in the course of his duty, he need not dread the climate more than if he were sent to the East or West Indies; and if he is engaged in trade he may be sure of making money as rapidly as in any place in the world, if he is a temperate, energetic man with his wits about him.

The great trials on the West Coast are the want of society, the difficulty of locomotion, and the difficulty of obtaining medical assistance when ill, at trading stations. It is to be hoped the public will not think all Africans are like the Fantees, or form their opinion of the nature of the country from the descriptions, by Special Correspondents, of the present abnormal state of the Gold Coast.

GRIFFIN AND CO, THE HARD, PORTSMOUTH, AND COCKSPUR STREET, LONDON, S.W.